THE POWER OF LISTENING

THE POWER OF LISTENING

Building Skills for Mission and Ministry

Lynne M. Baab

An Alban Institute Book

ROWMAN & LITTLEFIELD
Lanham • Boulder • New York • London

Published by Rowman & Littlefield
4501 Forbes Boulevard, Suite 200, Lanham, Maryland 20706
www.rowman.com

16 Carlisle Street, London W1D 3BT, United Kingdom

British Library Cataloguing in Publication Information Available

Library of Congress Cataloging-in-Publication Data

Baab, Lynne M.
The power of listening : building skills for mission and ministry / Lynne M. Baab.
p. cm.
Includes bibliographical references and index.
ISBN 978-1-56699-753-9 (cloth : alk. paper) — ISBN 978-1-56699-711-9 (pbk. : alk. paper) — ISBN 978-1-56699-712-6 (electronic)
1. Listening—Religious aspects—Christianity. I. Title.
BV4647.L56B33 2014
253'.7—dc23
2014004224

Printed in the United States of America

CONTENTS

Preface   vii
Acknowledgments   xiii

 1 A Call to Listen   1
 2 Listening to the Unspoken   15
 3 Listening within the Congregation   33
 4 Listening for Mission   51
 5 Listening in Consensus and Discernment   65
 6 Listening to God Together through Scripture   81
 7 Listening to God Together through Spiritual Practices   93
 8 The Listening Toolbox   107
 9 Anxiety and Listening   127
10 Humility and Listening   143
11 Listening, Receptivity, and Speaking Up   157

Notes   169
For Further Reading   177
About the Author   181

PREFACE

Our love for others is learning to listen to them.
—Dietrich Bonhoeffer, *Life Together*[1]

The minister of a small Presbyterian church told me, "We're failing in the wider church to listen to each other well. It's our central failing right now." Another minister said, "Listening is one of the biggest gifts we can give." Her perspective was echoed by a spiritual director who remarked, "Simply listening without comment is a powerful thing." A candidate for ordination noted, "What matters is the connection between people, and you can't have that unless you listen."

Daniel, a theological college lecturer who teaches evangelism, stressed the role of listening in evangelism and church planting. "We're coming to understand the centrality of listening. The danger is to think it's a part only of the beginning of the process, but the need for it continues." He advocated a repeating cycle in all forms of mission and ministry: listen—reflect—act—listen—reflect—act. Daniel's words echo the main point of this book that now, more than ever before, people committed to any form of ministry or mission need listening skills. People who lead congregations, those who serve others, and pioneers of new kinds of mission and ministry need to be able to listen to their team members, to the people in their congregation, and to the wider community. They also need to listen to God.

Much of the emphasis on listening in congregations has focused on pastoral care. Listening skills play a big role in training for Stephen Ministry,[2] healing prayer, and pastoral care teams. Listening as a part of caring ministries matters now as much as ever because personal needs are as complex, if not more complex, than in years past. Listening skills have also been emphasized for cross-cultural mission. I am convinced, however, that in these rapidly changing times, listening skills are essential for all forms of congregational ministry, in addition to pastoral care, and for all kinds of mission.

I view listening skills as essential tools for everything God asks us to do. Who God is, what the Holy Spirit is doing in the world, and Jesus' invitation to participate with him in mission and ministry must be at the center of all we do. In his 1989 book, *Answering God*, Eugene Peterson argues that prayers are tools, and he writes that tools

> are not the most important thing about us; God is: God in action creating, redeeming, and blessing. God makes the universe. God comes incarnate in Christ. God pours out his Spirit on creatures and creation. And tools are not the most evident thing about us; we are: the way our bodies function and our minds work, making love and making a living, our feelings of goodness and awfulness, asking questions about our origins and ends, sometimes believing and sometimes doubting the answers we receive. But in the business of being human, even though neither most important or most evident, tools are required.[3]

I agree with Peterson that the tools we use to nurture congregational life and mission are not ends in themselves. Tools must always remain subordinate to the goals they serve. But as Peterson indicates, tools do matter, and I want to encourage deliberate teaching of listening skills as valuable tools for all ministries within congregations and for all mission undertaken by individuals or congregations.

MY RESEARCH ON LISTENING

In 2011, I spent five months interviewing congregational leaders, both lay and ordained, about listening for the purpose of carrying out faithful, effective congregational ministry and mission. I focused my interviews on four topics: listening within the congregation, listening to the wider community, listening to God, and obstacles to listening. The interviews took place in the United States and the United Kingdom. My sixty-three interviewees came from a variety of denominations (listed in descending order of the number of interviewees from each denomination): Presbyterian Church (U.S.A.), Church of England, United Reformed Church, Church of Scotland, Southern Baptist Convention, Methodist Church of New Zealand, Methodist Church of Great Britain, United Church of Christ, and American Baptist Church U.S.A. Comments and stories from the interviews shaped this book and provided rich material about many aspects of listening. I have changed the names and identifying details of individuals and congregations.

This research was born out of the many books I have read about congregational life and mission, with emphases that include engaging with the local community, listening to God, and relationships as a source of congregational health. My research was also fueled by conversations with congregational leaders who are concerned about the future of the church in the West. Many of my interviewees expressed their belief that healthy congregations are composed of people who listen well. My interviewees pointed out that as the West moves deeper into a post-Christendom culture, the people coming into congregations, as well as the people in the wider community, are less likely to be operating from assumptions they share with each other or with the people already attending the congregation. With worldwide migration reshaping our communities and congregations, people in our neighborhoods, workplaces, and congregations bring diverse perspectives from their varied cultural and religious backgrounds. In order to understand how to minister in this changing world, my interviewees indicated that we need to know what people value and how they think. We need to understand what is going on inside the minds and hearts of the people we brush up against. Many writers focused on congregational mission today emphasize the necessity of paying attention to the local community, watching for God's presence and action already there. These writers encourage congregations to partner with the Holy Spirit, who is already working in the communities beyond the walls of the church. This kind of paying attention requires the ability to listen, and I believe seminaries and congregations fall short because we seldom affirm or teach those skills for the purposes of congregational mission. Most of my interviewees agreed with this premise.

In addition, changing economic realities have created profound pastoral care needs. As noted above, pastoral care has long been a focus of listening training. One interviewee mentioned the new employment patterns that mean some people will be underemployed or unemployed for years and even decades, which creates significant inner turmoil and identity issues in the people affected, and this is only one example of the kind of pastoral care needs that require listening skills today. In addition, my interviewees talked about other societal trends that emphasize listening as appropriate in our time. We are faced with unprecedented challenges from new communication technologies, which raise significant questions about how relationships work in online settings and what forms of "listening" are appropriate online. Polarization over many issues has increased the distance between people both inside and outside of congregations. Some of that polarization might be reduced if people learned to listen for the purpose of understanding others' views, while at the same time affirming that listening and understanding do not imply agreement. Many books on communication in congregations stress the increased significance of storytelling in small groups and congregations in our postmodern times, which is another reason listening matters today. If we are going to honor the stories people tell about their journeys of faith, someone needs to be listening. All of the societal and congregational factors mentioned by my interviewees make listening an urgent task for congregations today. In the face of these challenges and changes, loving listening encourages connection and depth, which contribute to life and health for individuals and congregations.

Listening to God is another aspect of listening that is gaining attention in our time. My interviewees noted that many congregational leaders have become weary of thinking about church as a business. Many are looking for authentic experiences of God's guidance through consensus building and communal discernment, rather than through leadership and decision-making models shaped by business or government. Becoming a better listener to the people in our lives can help us grow in the ability to listen for God's voice, and the converse is often true as well. Learning to listen for God's voice helps us pay attention to the voices of the people around us. In chapters 5 to 7 I will discuss the place of communal listening to God in consensus and discernment, in Scripture, and through spiritual practices.

To my surprise, my interviewees were most animated and passionate when they discussed obstacles to listening. The interviewees indicated that many people lack the skills to listen, perhaps because they have never experienced good listening themselves or because they have never been taught basic skills. Many of my interviewees, as well as the experts I consulted, agreed that the ability to listen well is a skill that can be learned. Therefore I have dedicated chapter 8 to a toolbox of skills that good listeners draw on, and chapters 9 and 10 focus on overcoming obstacles to listening. I have arranged the chapters in an order that seems to flow well, but each chapter can stand on its own. I want to encourage you, if you are drawn to a particular aspect of listening, to begin by reading the chapters that interest you most.

The New Testament letter of James advocates that we be quick to listen (James 1:19). I hope and pray that this book will encourage you to think about listening skills as valuable tools for mission and ministry. I hope you will be motivated to teach the material in this book in your congregations, and I hope the result will be congregations whose communal life is characterized by careful, respectful, and loving listening. I hope that the wider community will perceive that the people of your congregation listen and understand, even when they do not agree. I hope that nurturing listening skills will enable you, and the members of your congregation, to open your hearts to receive love and grace from God and precious gifts from the people in your lives; listening helps us to receive from others and from God in unexpected, rich, and rewarding ways. I hope that growing in your ability to listen will help you speak more effectively and with greater love at the right time. I hope and pray that you will find a quality of holiness in your listening as you experiment with the skills presented in this book and ponder the patterns of listening discussed.

ACKNOWLEDGMENTS

First and foremost, I want to thank the sixty-three people who talked with me in formal interviews about listening. I could not have written this book without you. I promised you anonymity, so I cannot list your names here, but I want to extend my warm thanks for the time and thoughts you gave to me.

In late 2012 and early 2013, when I was writing this book, many friends and colleagues conversed with me about listening. In addition, in those months I presented material related to this book in numerous settings: the Anglican Diocesan Ministry Educators' annual meeting in Dunedin, the Anglican Bishops' conference in Dunedin, the Australasian Academy of Homiletics conference in Sydney, the Australia New Zealand Association for Theological Schools conference in Auckland, a seminar in the Department of Theology and Religion at the University of Otago in Dunedin, and at my women writers' group. In all those settings, the discussion shaped my thoughts, and I am very grateful for the interaction and ideas.

Jayme and Erinn Koerselman were invaluable conversion partners about obstacles to listening. Jayme, who teaches counseling at Laidlaw College in Auckland, gave me a framework for understanding the role of anxiety in blocking our ability to listen, and Erinn, also a counselor, contributed numerous illustrations. Thank you, Jayme and Erinn.

Another helpful conversation partner as I wrote this book was Julie Christensen, a thoughtful and wise listener and a close friend who has supported me through ups and downs for more than twenty years. Thank you, Julie, for all you are to me.

This is my fifth book with editor extraordinaire Beth Ann Gaede. Beth, you help me improve my writing in so many ways, and you are a wonderful conversation partner on so many topics. Thank you for your excellent editing help and your friendship.

I also want to thank the many people who have listened to me. My husband Dave has spent countless (endless?) hours listening to my ups and downs, and Dave has been a frequent conversation partner about the characteristics of good listeners. Thank you, beloved Dave. I have also received so much love and listening time from my brother Mark, the two therapists who helped me navigate my years of depression, the three spiritual directors who helped me grow in seeing God's hand in my life, and numerous friends who have listened to my ramblings. To everyone who has listened to me, thank you. My life has been enriched because of the support and encouragement that came through your listening.

All quotations from the Bible are from the New Revised Standard Version. All stories are told with permission. Names of individuals and churches, as well as some identifying details, have been changed.

1

A CALL TO LISTEN

You must understand this, my beloved: let everyone be quick to listen.
—James 1:19

Eileen spent most her twenties teaching in India, where she also served as a lay leader in a congregation with strong community ministries. She returned to her hometown, Smithville, right before her thirtieth birthday. Her home church, Smithville Community Church, welcomed her back with open arms.

In the years Eileen was away, the church had experienced a painful split, leaving the congregation with twenty-five members, a building, and only enough money to pay the minister part time. Congregation members saw the energy and enthusiasm that Eileen brought back from her time overseas, and they asked her to take on a lay leadership position in the dispirited congregation.

Eileen believes that life and vitality in a congregation come from engagement with God's heart. By this she means a concern for God's priorities and values, a focus on the needs of the world that are close to God's heart, and a willingness to consider where and how the Gospel can address those needs. Eileen was influenced by her time in India, where her exposure to Christians from all over the world caused her faith to grow in unexpected ways. Eileen thinks all congregations, no matter how small, need to participate in local, national, and global mission in some way. In her early months back in Smithville, she prayed that the congregation would discover opportunities to take part in mission in all three areas, and she encouraged the congregation members to pray with her.

As she listened to the members' concerns and passions, and as they prayed together, it seemed to Eileen that an overseas mission trip might raise the energy level of the congregation by challenging members to serve God in new ways and by enabling them to see God at work in new places. She began to put out feelers in the congregation about an overseas trip. Would some people be interested in travelling to Malawi with her to visit a missionary couple with ties to Smithville? The answer seemed to be "yes."

While interest in the mission trip was ramping up, and while congregation members were organizing various fundraising projects, Eileen encouraged members to listen to local needs as well. Having been back in the congregation for several months, she knew that overseas mission would not be enough to get them reconnected with the power and joy of the Good News in Jesus Christ. She believed they needed to learn to see and meet local needs as well, because they would be energized by seeing God's work in people's lives right in their community.

Eileen encouraged congregation members to try to ask questions whenever they had a conversation with people in the community, and she encouraged them to pray for perception as they listened. What needs did people in the town experience that weren't being met? What concerns did the congregation members hear as they talked with residents of Smithville?

One listening opportunity occurred during the fundraisers for the Malawi trip. The congregation held several sales of donated items, and many residents of Smithville attended the sales. Members of the church engaged the shoppers in conversation, asking questions about the shoppers' own needs and the shoppers' concerns about their town and region.

In congregational prayer times, members prayed that God would guide their listening and their perception about what they heard. Eileen encouraged them to ask themselves three questions as they pondered what they heard in conversations, and as they prayed individually and communally in response to what they heard:

- What's your passion?
- What burns on your heart?
- Why are you here?

These questions enabled congregation members to think about their own energies, interests, and concerns as they pondered their conversations in the local community. These questions also encouraged members to listen to God's nudges inside them and to examine the focus of their own energy, because their energy and enthusiasm might indicate God's guidance for them.

They would need to draw on their energy and enthusiasm as they undertook new forms of ministry to their community. They discussed the other resources they had, including their building. Eileen encouraged them to listen to each other carefully as they discussed the resources they believed they had to offer, the needs in the community, and where they felt God was leading them. She believed that prayer and discussion about all these factors would help the congregation to discern God's guidance for them as a community.

After months of listening, pondering, and praying, several congregation members reported that they felt a burden for mothers of young children who felt isolated and lacked support. So the congregation began praying about the possibility of establishing a preschool in their building, the kind of preschool where the parents are involved. They wanted the parents to be able to build relationships with each other, not simply drop off their children.

Plans for the preschool developed alongside the trip to Malawi. The preschool got up and running, and several congregation members volunteered there so they could get to know the parents. As relationships developed between the congregation members and the parents, many of the congregation's volunteers realized that some of the parents had very little knowledge of the Christian faith, and some of them were interested in learning more. The clarity of that need resulted in an Alpha course.[1] Alpha involves a dinner, a video about the basics of the Christian faith, and a discussion. The dinners and discussions became further opportunities to listen to local needs and concerns.

Further listening revealed that some of the parents at the preschool and some of the people attending Alpha were experiencing challenges in their marriages. Alpha offers a marriage enrichment course as well as a basic introduction to Christianity, and the congregation decided to offer Marriage Alpha. The two courses, Alpha and Marriage Alpha, were offered once or twice a year for several years.

The congregation was also instrumental in establishing Smithville's first food bank, as food needs in the wider community became evident in the economic downturn. After a couple of years, Smithville's food bank became affiliated with a national food bank organization, which made Eileen smile, because their food bank ministry now had national connections. The congregation was now connected with global, local, and national mission, because after that first trip to Malawi, overseas mission trips every year or two had continued.

Eight years after Eileen's return to Smithville, her congregation had about a hundred members. Some of them had come to faith in Christ through Alpha or Marriage Alpha. Some of them were new people who had moved into the community. The congregation was again able to pay its minister for full-time work. The congregation was still not large, but members were involved in significant local ministry, and they still took trips overseas. Eileen believes these forms of mission give life to the congregation, and she is proud of their productive and generous service to their community.

Eileen urged her congregation to pray for God's guidance for mission, and she encouraged several forms of listening to provide fuel for that prayer. She encouraged members to listen to people in the community beyond the congregation in order to hear their needs. She encouraged members to listen for God's guidance and to pay attention to their own energy and passion as they pondered what they had heard in the community. And she encouraged congregation members to listen to each other as they processed what they had heard in the community and from God, and as they discussed the resources they believed they had to meet the needs they perceived.

WHY DO WE LISTEN?

Humans listen for many different reasons. Like most mammals, birds, and reptiles, humans listen at a very basic level to protect ourselves and our loved ones from danger. For a raccoon or robin, listening brings awareness of predators. When I ride my bicycle, I pay attention to the car and truck traffic on the road, and part of my awareness comes from listening. When I had young children and I walked with them near busy streets, I used all my senses, including hearing, to try to keep them safe from harm.

Listening plays a role for some animals in their ability to find food, and a parallel for humans might involve all the listening we do that gives us information we need to feed ourselves and to thrive physically. Some of this listening focuses on simple facts, but we listen for many different kinds of information. Where is cheese located in this supermarket? How much does cheddar cheese cost? What are the nutritional issues related to eating cheese? Can people who are lactose intolerant eat cheese?

As we listen for information, we easily move from facts to analysis of the facts, and then to deeper meaning. Note the progression in complexity and level of meaning in the following series of questions: What time does that movie start? Where is the theater located? What kinds of things are reviewers saying about the movie? Does it sound like a good movie? Does this movie have spiritual implications? If I took a group of high school students from the youth group to that movie, what kinds of issues might we discuss afterward?

Communication scholars make a distinction between hearing and listening. Hearing involves perceiving a sound with the ear, while listening involves paying attention to the sounds received by the ear and perceiving the meaning in them. In congregations, hearing is an issue that often needs to be addressed, perhaps by providing better sound systems, hearing loupes for the hearing impaired, sound deadening in gathering spaces, and sound-proofing for offices where confidential conversations take place. Particularly in congregations with aging members, paying attention to issues of hearing bears good fruit. This book, however, focuses on listening, the process of giving meaning to the sounds we hear.

We might say listening involves being alert to the sounds we hear. When we listen, we heed the sounds, tune into them, give consideration to them, or process them actively. In fact, the English word "listen" comes from two Anglo-Saxon words. One of them means "hearing," and the other means "to wait in suspense."[2] Conversations might manifest greater love and attentiveness if we adopted an attitude of waiting in suspense to learn something from the other person's words.

In common parlance, we interchange the meaning of these two words—listen and hear—quite frequently. "Yes, I hear you," we might say when we want to indicate that we're listening carefully. Or we might say, "I'm listening to the radio," when we're immersed in another task and the radio has become background noise only. However, for the purposes of discussing listening in congregations, I want to differentiate between these two words. Hearing involves perceiving sounds, and listening involves paying attention to what we hear.

To illustrate this distinction further, imagine that you and I are riding bicycles together. Using "hear" to mean perceiving sounds with the ear, you and I either hear the noise of the truck coming up behind us, or we don't. If we do hear it, each of us will give it an interpretation, and perhaps our interpretations will differ. We may disagree about whether or not the truck is source of danger. Even in the relatively straightforward situation of discerning the danger inherent in a sound, each of us will interpret what we hear.

When I take the youth group to that new movie and we talk about it afterward, I will hear the words that come out of the mouths of the youth group members, but will I truly listen to what they are saying? Will I hear the emotions behind the words? Will Liam's intensity and loud voice irritate me so much that I don't listen deeply and carefully to his emotions or opinions? Will Sandie refer to her parents' divorce for the hundredth time, and in a whining tone, so I don't listen well to her? And what interpretation will I give to the words I hear? Many factors impede our ability to listen carefully, even if we are physically hearing the words people say. In chapters 9 and 10, I will present obstacles to listening that are common in congregations. Confronting those obstacles results in a quantum improvement in listening.

The challenges of interpretation grow more intense when conversations focus on deeper issues, when the purpose of listening becomes more nuanced. Why might I desire to listen deeply to the youth group members when discussing a movie with spiritual themes? Is the goal to help the students feel that someone cares about their thoughts? To help them make deeper connections to Christian themes? To motivate them to draw near to God in prayer? And to what extent am I accurately perceiving the central issues the students are trying to talk about, particularly when I have a goal or agenda for the conversation?

When Eileen's congregation held a bake sale to raise money for a mission trip and someone stopped to chat after purchasing some cookies, what motivations were driving the listener? What was the purpose of listening to the shopper? To get information about what they were thinking and feeling about the needs they experienced in their life? To understand what they perceived to be the needs of their community? To help them feel like someone was listening with empathy, which might convey acceptance or caring from that individual or perhaps even from the church or from God?

When we are listening carefully, we are usually paying attention on many different levels. Let's imagine that the person purchasing some cookies at the bake sale at Eileen's church was talking about a traffic accident that recently occurred at the intersection near the church building. The person listening might be simultaneously taking in the details of the accident and the emotions of the person telling the story. The listener might also hear concerns about the number of accidents that happen at that intersection, and she might wonder if some action should be taken to make the intersection safer. Which aspect should the listener pay attention to? To the facts? To the emotions of the person telling the story? To the strategic implications? Can we listen to all those things simultaneously?

THE PURPOSES OF LISTENING IN CONGREGATIONS

When ordained ministers are trained in listening skills in seminary or continuing education courses, most often the stated purpose is to offer pastoral care, pastoral counseling, or spiritual direction. When lay people are trained in listening skills, perhaps through a program such as Stephen Ministry, the goal is usually to equip them to provide care for people in emotional or spiritual need. Pastoral care listening dominates the books, seminars, and resources on listening skills related to congregational ministry. Pastoral care listening usually focuses on the kind of listening that lets people know someone cares about their situation. Listening to someone patiently and carefully is a great gift, and compassionate listening communicates love and acceptance, so this emphasis is appropriate.

Many people of faith view deep and careful listening as an end in itself, and in many situations that is true. When someone listens carefully to us, it helps us feel as if our lives matter. When we are in the midst of any kind of trauma and pain, perceiving that someone understands what we're going through usually feels like balm to the soul. In the midst of irritation or frustration, sometimes our negative emotions lift if we can tell someone about the situation and how we feel. In addition, a good listener can help us talk through an issue we're facing, often with the result that we are able to come up with an appropriate solution that fits with our own values, priorities, and resources.

The kind of listening that communicates understanding and acceptance, and that helps us come up with our own solutions, has implications for mission. Christians are called to be in the world as Jesus was in the world, so it is worth noting that Jesus was a champion listener. A few examples include his interactions with Nicodemus in John 3:1–21, the woman at the well in John 4, and the woman who had bled for many years in Mark 5:21–43. The gift of a listening ear communicates love and grace, qualities found abundantly in Jesus. Careful listening is often the most appropriate way, within or outside a congregation, to show love and to communicate that God is love.

Careful and deep listening, however, is not enough when people have practical needs that we could help meet. Jesus, the One who loves, listened carefully but also addressed practical and societal issues. When Jesus healed the ten lepers (Luke 17:11–19), he sent them to the local priest, because he knew that the priest would certify them as healed, which would allow them to be restored to their community. Jesus listened simultaneously on several levels. He listened to needs for healing and needs for relationship, and in his actions he responded to the variety of needs he heard.

Effective listening for ministry and mission today involves listening on multiple levels like Jesus did. When the members of Smithville Community Church asked questions of people in the preschool, at Alpha, at bake sales, and elsewhere in the wider community, they undoubtedly began with listening to the individual's needs. Sometimes they probably focused simply on conveying to the speaker that someone cared about their feelings. Sometimes they undoubtedly simply drew out the person who was sharing a need or a concern. Sometimes they probably watched for patterns as the speaker talked about needs in the wider community. In some instances they may have known of a resource that would help that person at that moment, and they undoubtedly steered the person toward that resource.

They were also trying to listen to God at the same time they were listening to people, hoping to discern God's presence and God's guidance related to that specific person and to the patterns of need in the community. Many good listeners talk about "double listening," which in this case involved trying to listen simultaneously to a person and to God. Eileen had asked the congregation members to pray for the ability to perceive God's guidance and presence as they listened to the wider community. Perceiving where God is at work depends on the work of the Holy Spirit within us. Eileen had also asked them to ponder their own inner desires. Our own passions and sense of purpose are part of the way God gives us direction and speaks to us.

Effective listening for congregations today also involves listening to each other in the community of faith as we talk through what we believe we have heard from the wider community and from God. In addition, we need to discuss the resources we believe we have at our disposal. Often in a discussion, as I listen to the perspectives of others, I see things so differently because of what the other people say. I might see new resources I didn't know we had. Something I heard in the wider community is illuminated or put into perspective because of someone else's insights. God's nudging in my heart seems more significant when someone else reports the same interest. In our communities of faith, we rely on each other to gain wisdom and perspective in many areas, and listening plays an important role in that process.

SOME HELPFUL VOCABULARY

Three phrases have helped me think creatively about listening in my own personal life, as well as listening in a congregational context. The phrases are "holy listening," "holy curiosity," and "receptivity." Sometimes evocative vocabulary opens up new ways to think about an issue, and these three phrases have done that for me.

Holy Listening

Congregational consultant and seminary professor Craig Satterlee uses the term "holy listening" to describe the kind of listening we do when we seek to discern "the presence and activity of God in the joys, struggles, and hopes of the ordinary activities of congregational life, as well as the uncertainty and opportunity of change and transition."[3]

This kind of listening is holy because when we engage in it, we are hoping and expecting to encounter God. Leaders and members of a congregation can listen in a holy manner in a variety of places and activities, as Satterlee describes so vividly. He believes holy listening is indispensible, because it builds intimacy in congregations and helps people connect with each other in a way that goes beyond the superficial, resulting in powerful bonds between people. I believe the kinds of listening to the wider community described in this book can be considered holy listening as well.

Satterlee notes that our listening is imperfect, because we are flawed people with our own agendas, but we can try to listen attentively and carefully. He writes:

> Holy listening demands vigilance, alertness, openness to others, and the expectation that God will speak through them. Holy listening trusts that the Holy Spirit acts in and through our listening. We discern and discover the wisdom and will of God by listening to one another and to ourselves. From a Christian perspective, holy listening also takes the incarnation seriously; it dares to believe that, as God was enfleshed in Jesus of Nazareth, so God is embodied in other people and in the things around us. [4]

I love the idea that holy listening takes the incarnation seriously. My understanding of God's call to mission is rooted in a commitment to honor the incarnation of Jesus by responding to Jesus' words that we are sent into the world as he was sent (John 17:18). As we do that, the Holy Spirit enables us to perceive the presence of Jesus in wildly diverse people and places, and our listening becomes holy.

Holy Curiosity

Another helpful and thought-provoking term is "holy curiosity," coined by Albert Einstein in the 1940s to describe the freedom of inquiry he considered to be important in science education. [5] People of faith have adopted this phrase because it evokes so much about effective Christian ministry. In order to meet needs, we must be curious about what they are. In order to give aid or help, we need to be curious about the ways to do it most effectively and in forms that empower the recipient. Our curiosity needs to have a holy quality about it, centered in God's gentle and insightful love.

Two recent books use Einstein's phrase in their title in ways that complement the themes of this book. Pastor and blogger Winn Collier has written a book, *Holy Curiosity*,[6] which focuses on the way Jesus used questions. Collier argues that Jesus often refused to give people direct and detailed answers. Instead, he asked questions that proved to be life changing. For me, Jesus' loving and provocative interactions with people, described in the four Gospels, have been significant models as I have tried to grow as a listener. Reading the Gospels with an eye to Jesus the communicator—the listener, the question asker—is instructive in many ways, as Collier advises and as I have experienced.

Psychology professor Amy Hollingsworth also wrote a book entitled *Holy Curiosity*,[7] which addresses creativity. Hollingsworth believes that creativity is not possible without a kind of holy curiosity, including listening to our own lives to see the patterns and possibilities there. Sometimes people of faith have an innate aversion to paying attention to their own lives because such an endeavor seems self-absorbed. Eileen's leadership in her congregation, described at the beginning of this chapter, illustrates the significance of engaging in holy curiosity about ourselves, however. Eileen asked the congregation members to ponder three questions— What's your passion? What burns on your heart? Why are you here?— that encourage reflection on personal thoughts and feelings. These questions require a kind of holy curiosity about our inner realities. That kind of reflection helps us understand what energizes us and what will give us the power and passion to take part in ministry for the long term.

The term "holy curiosity," like "holy listening," can help us ponder ways to love incarnationally in our world. We certainly need creative new ways to minister in a rapidly changing world, and Amy Hollingsworth is right that creativity is not possible without holy curiosity. Creativity is fed by our fascination with the quirky, astonishing, unexpected, and sometimes baffling world that God created, an amazing world that includes such a wide diversity of people with their own priorities and passions. Am I willing to engage in holy curiosity with my new Muslim, Hindu, or Buddhist neighbors, asking what they value and care about? Am I willing to practice holy curiosity with the long-term unemployed person in my congregation, asking how I can pray for her? Am I willing to listen carefully to others and to my own inner voice with a kind of curiosity informed by Jesus' care, attention, and creative communication patterns?

Can holy curiosity play a role in discussions within the congregation about where to go and what to do in congregational ministry?

Receptivity

Ten or fifteen years ago I noticed that some people pray with their hands facing upward, as if they are trying to catch or receive something as they pray. I began to experiment with that posture when I pray as well. I find opening my hands nurtures an inner attitude of receptivity, a willingness to receive from God whatever God wants to give. In recent years, I have consciously and frequently prayed that I will grow in receptivity. Trying to be more receptive to God and to others has had a significant impact in my life. I have always been quite self-directed and proactive, and I've learned with age that many of the good gifts of life do not come from my initiative. Instead those gifts are simply there; they appear in my life. I want to do a better job noticing and receiving them.

One of those gifts is the diversity of people, the astonishing variety of personalities, opinions, beliefs, and values that we find in others if we pay attention. Part of how we receive glimpses of that astonishing diversity is through listening. A receptive posture helps us listen to others and to God more deeply, with holy curiosity. And as we practice listening to God and as we pay attention to the passions and priorities of others through careful listening, we become more receptive to all that life has to offer.

In the closing chapter of this book, I will return to the three phrases I have discussed here—holy listening, holy curiosity, and receptivity—and will look at them a second time in light of the intervening chapters. All three phrases urge an attitude of respect, interest, and willingness to interact with the concerns of others, so I encourage you to keep them in mind as you read.

QUESTIONS FOR REFLECTION, JOURNALING, AND GROUP DISCUSSION

- Name one or two of the best listeners you know. What listening skills do you see them using? What attitudes and inner convictions do you think lie behind their ability to listen well?

- What did you learn about listening from your family of origin? What skills and attitudes have you kept and developed from your family? What have you changed?
- Think about your congregation. In what settings do people listen to each other? In what ways have you seen your congregation listen to the wider community? In what ways is listening to God affirmed for individuals and for groups?
- Do any of the terms used at the end of this chapter—holy listening, holy curiosity, receptivity—resonate with you? Do any of them help you think about listening in a new light? Write a prayer for yourself using one of those terms.
- This week, pay someone a compliment for the way he or she listens to you. Ask about the factors that encouraged listening skills.

2

LISTENING TO THE UNSPOKEN

If you are at all typical, listening takes up more of your waking hours than any other activity. A study of persons of varied occupational backgrounds showed that 70 percent of their waking moments were spent in communication. And of that time, writing took 9 percent, reading absorbed 16 percent, talking accounted for 30 percent, and listening occupied 45 percent.
—Robert Bolton, "Listening Is More Than Merely Hearing"[1]

In my first preaching course in seminary, more than twenty-five years ago, we talked about the famous idea from Karl Barth that as preachers prepare their sermons, they should hold a Bible in one hand and a newspaper in the other. I took it to mean that we must be aware of societal trends as well as breaking news events when we prepare sermons, so that we can show the ways biblical priorities address the concerns that occupy the minds and hearts of people in the pews.

Later I found out that Barth argued that the Bible must have priority in listening. He believed the current events and trends in the newspaper must be viewed and interpreted through the lens of the Bible.[2] John Stott makes a similar point when he talks about "double listening." He writes that preachers know they need to listen to the Word of God, but they are often less aware that they also need to listen to the world. And, he notes, listening to the world is often uncomfortable:

For the voices of our contemporaries may take the form of shrill and strident protest. They are now querulous, now appealing, now aggressive in tone. There are also the anguished cries of those who are suffering, and the pain, doubt, anger, alienation and even despair of those who are estranged from God. I am not suggesting that we should listen to God and to our fellow human beings in the same way or with the same degree of deference. We listen to the Word with humble reverence, anxious to understand it, and resolved to believe and obey what we come to understand. We listen to the world with critical alertness, anxious to understand it too, and resolved not necessarily to believe and obey it, but to sympathize with it and to seek grace to discover how the gospel relates to it. [3]

Both Barth and Stott were discussing preaching, but their views are relevant for mission and ministry as well. Congregational leaders need to pay attention to the trends of the wider culture, and they need to listen to the specific concerns in the congregation and the local community. The purpose of all that listening, Stott says, is to sympathize and also to seek the grace to figure out the way the Gospel relates to what we see and hear. As we engage in double listening, as we study the Bible but also listen to the needs of people, some of that listening will involve focusing on spoken words. Some of it will involve attentiveness to newspapers and other news media, entertainment media, social media, and all the ways people communicate these days. Some of it will involve listening to nonverbal communication in personal conversations, which includes body language, facial expression, and tone of voice.

In the quotation at the beginning of this chapter, communication consultant Robert Bolton cites research indicating that people, on average, spend 70 percent of their days communicating. Bolton notes that 45 percent of our communication time involves listening, and another 16 percent involves reading. I consider reading to be a form of listening because when we read we are focusing on interpreting the meaning communicated by the writer. If we include reading as a form of listening, then well over half of our time spent communicating is spent listening, and a significant portion of listening involves attention to things unspoken.

In chapter 1 I indicated that the root of the word "listening" lies in two Anglo-Saxon words that mean "hearing" and "to wait in suspense." Much of chapter 1 made the case that listening involves giving meaning to the sounds we hear. However, listening for mission and ministry also includes paying attention to and giving meaning to forms of communication that do not involve sounds. This means noticing and interpreting things unspoken, which includes attentiveness to body language, discussed further in chapter 8, as well as to written words, news and entertainment media, and online communication.

When John Stott argued in 1992 for double listening, he encouraged the reader to pay attention to the voices of contemporaries and the anguished cries of people in need. He was undoubtedly thinking of the actual voices of people he talked with in his role as minister at All Soul's Church in London, people both within and outside the congregation. He was probably also thinking of news stories—on television and in newspapers—about people in need in other parts of the world, as well as books that expressed people's needs and desires. Today we might hear those voices and cries in many more forms than in 1992:

- in face-to-face conversations
- on television
- in newspapers printed on paper or read online
- in books
- in blog posts
- in posts on social networking sites such as Facebook, Twitter, or Linked-In
- on other websites such as photo sharing sites or special interest sites
- in online discussion forums
- in emails
- in cell phone text messages

In these diverse places we listen to the spoken and unspoken communication of our contemporaries. In these diverse places we also pay attention to verbal and nonverbal communication. Most of this book focuses on listening to spoken speech, but unspoken communication also has great significance, including messages that might be verbal (involving words) or nonverbal (involving body language, images, and observation of many other components of people's lives that communicate their values and priorities). The distinctions between these forms of communication can be helpful in understanding the ways and places we listen. Verbal communication—communication with words—takes many forms, including conversations, speeches, radio news, novels, magazine articles, and 140-character Twitter posts. Verbal communication can be divided into two categories: spoken/heard or written. When we read articles in the local

newspaper as a way of listening to our community, we are paying attention to verbal communication that is unspoken. When we look at the
pictures in the local newspaper, we are paying attention nonverbal communication, messages that do not involve words, which are also unspok-
en.

UNSPOKEN COMMUNICATION IN CONGREGATIONS

Unspoken communication in congregations includes many of the ways
members and visitors express their priorities and concerns. What activities in the congregation do people choose to participate in? Where do
congregation members volunteer in the community? What charities do
they give to beyond the church? What does the foyer of the church building look like, and what does it communicate? What does the children's
committee post on its bulletin board? What kinds of graphics are used in
the worship bulletin, and what do the fonts communicate? What style are
the banners in the worship space, and what images are used? These are
forms of communication that can be observed. We might accurately say
we are listening to them, even though spoken words are not involved. The
patterns of these activities and communication play a role in forming the
fabric of a congregation.

Increasingly, unspoken communication in congregations involves the
online world. George, a man in his sixties, attends a Baptist congregation
with lots of university students and young adults. Several of the young
adults in his congregation have friended George on Facebook. George
follows their Facebook posts quite conscientiously, because he knows the
posts provide a window into what they are thinking about. He often posts
an encouraging word in response to concerns they express, and he prays
frequently for the situations described in the Facebook posts: job interviews, challenges at the university or at work, and their marriages and
relationships. He looks at the photos they post as further fuel for prayer.

On Sunday mornings, George seldom converses with these Facebook
friends. He can see that they are talking with their age-mates, although
they will often give him a wave or a smile. George is committed to
nurturing the well-being and spiritual growth of the young adults in his
congregation, partly because he has grown to care about them from their
Facebook posts, and partly because he knows how hard it is for young

adults to follow Jesus in this consumerist, self-focused culture. Facebook allows him to pray for them with some knowledge of their situation. George listens to the young adults in his congregation, yet that listening seldom involves spoken words.

My husband, Dave, volunteers with a ministry to international students at the university where I teach. This ministry has set up a Facebook group, which is helpful for posting times and locations of meetings and social gatherings. When the Facebook group was established about three years ago, Dave viewed it mostly as a means for publicizing events. Now he sees the relational benefit as well. Students who have returned to their home country post prayer requests on the page as they graduate from the university and look for jobs or as they deal with other challenges. Students past and present post good news. Initially, my husband was slower than I was to spend much time on Facebook, but he now looks at it far more often than I do, because it connects him with his students so profoundly.

Other forms of social media, including Twitter and Pinterest, provide opportunities to learn about the activities and concerns of people inside and outside congregations. Blogs do the same. I think every minister should consider having a blog in order to express thoughts and concerns in a casual way. In addition, I think congregational leaders should make an effort to follow the blogs of people in their congregations. Blog posts often provide a window into people's thoughts and feelings. Online photo sharing also gives an insight into concerns and priorities. Much photo sharing happens on Facebook, but some people use websites such as Flickr that are devoted primarily to photos, and those photos give a glimpse into their lives. Pinterest is another website that provides unspoken messages about what people consider to be important.

UNSPOKEN COMMUNICATION BEYOND THE CONGREGATION

Keeping in touch with concerns and issues in the local community requires a focus on both spoken and unspoken communication. Several of my interviewees talked about the importance of knowing the neighbors on their street and taking the time to chat when shopping in local businesses. Others talked about the significance of the local section of city newspapers, as well as neighborhood newspapers, as a way to keep up to date on the priorities and concerns of people in the local community. Several interviewees talked about Facebook and Twitter as a way they keep in touch with issues local people are facing. Some interviewees talked about the value of knowing what goes on at local gathering places. They advocated observing the various ethnic groups and immigrant groups that are present in communities and accessing demographic studies of communities. The websites of local organizations can give a glimpse of what they are up to.

Chapter 4 will focus on listening beyond the congregation and will provide many examples of listening that involves spoken words. Congregational leaders can listen to their local communities through paying attention to many forms of unspoken communication as well, including printed and online communication that gives information about what's happening locally. Some of those events and some of that information can help congregations know how to engage with their local community. An example of that kind of listening comes from the neighborhood in which I live, a long narrow valley that extends from the north edge of our city. The valley has a lot of houses approaching a hundred years in age, many of which have not been updated very much. That means they are extremely difficult to heat in the winter because they lack insulation and double-pane windows. Demographic maps of the city show that a fair number of the families living in those older houses are low income, so they lack the resources to upgrade their houses.

A few years ago the government initiated a subsidy program to help lower-income people insulate their houses. One of the churches in the valley established a group of volunteers from their own church and other local churches to help families access the money available from the government. This group helped families assess the insulation needs in their home, helped arrange for the contractors to install the insulation, and served as advocates for families if they had trouble getting payment from the government.

That project was born from a lot of listening to unspoken information, including demographic charts of the neighborhood and observation of the age of the houses in the valley. Undoubtedly some of the impetus for that project came from conversations with people who live in the valley and talked at church, in local clubs, or shops about how cold their houses were. Listening to the blend of spoken and unspoken information impelled mission.

LISTENING THROUGH THE VISUAL ARTS

The visual arts provide another window into the concerns of the local community. A congregation in a major city holds an Abrahamic faiths art exhibit each year. They contact the Jewish, Muslim, and Christian communities in the city and ask for visual art submissions that express the unique characteristics of each religion. The organizers of the exhibition are adamant that they don't want to focus on the values the three faiths share in common. Instead, they want to highlight the uniqueness of each of the Abrahamic faiths, so people who attend the exhibition can grow in awareness and understanding of others. The minister of the congregation that hosts the art exhibition said that it has made a significant contribution to improved relationships between Christians, Jews, and Muslims in their city.

Visual art is a nonverbal and unspoken form of communication that speaks profoundly. Spoken conversations have arisen because of the exhibition, but unspoken conversations, while people look at the art, have occurred as well because viewers of visual art listen to and perceive the values of the artist. Two congregations in my city have held art exhibitions. One of them featured the work of artists and crafts people from within the congregation, and looking at what they had made gave me a glimpse into the values and priorities of those individuals. The other congregation invited contributions from the wider community. The quality of the art was quite good, and the subjects chosen for the paintings and photographs gave me a sense of what people in my city see as they look around the community. More congregations are engaging with various forms of visual art in our time because of the significant communication that happens, both spoken and unspoken.

A congregation in a major city has a juried art exhibition each year focused on spirituality in art, open to artists both inside and outside the congregation, with a cash prize awarded by a jury. When the congregational leaders first got the idea for this art display, they were concerned that very few pieces would be submitted. To their surprise, every year they have had dozens of submissions. The paintings, photographs, collages, and sculptures submitted to the art exhibition speak about what each artist considers to be significant about spirituality. The people who attend the exhibition listen to a variety of voices, yet words and sounds are not used.

On the weekend the show opens, the congregation holds an arts festival, with lots of hand-on art projects that allow visitors to participate in the creation of art. The congregation is located on a busy street, and some of the hands-on projects take place on the sidewalk in front of the church, so passers-by can join in. One year a sculptor brought in a large piece of marble. The sculptor laid out the shape and design for a sculpture to be made from the marble block. On the weekend of the arts festival, the chunk of marble was put on the sidewalk, and congregation members and members of the wider community were invited to chip away at the marble, following the design planned by the sculptor. When the sculpture was finished, it was placed at the front of the congregation's worship space as an object of art but also as a visual representation of the involvement of the congregation members and members of the wider community in creating it. That sculpture speaks. The people who see it are invited to listen to what it says about the ways people can work together.

EXEGETING CULTURE

Engagement with the visual arts and visual artists plays an increasing role in congregations today, and visual arts enable the kind of listening to the unspoken that I'm describing in this chapter: listening to the priorities, cries, concerns, and passions of people both inside and outside congregations. The concerns of people both inside and outside congregations can also be heard in movies, television programs, novels, video games, popular songs, and advertisements. Trends of the wider society often take their shape from, and are reflected in, the global entertainment and advertising culture, which influences the way we understand so many aspects of everyday life, including money, possessions, work, sexuality, our homes, and our bodies. The phrase "exegeting culture" is sometimes used to describe a process of analyzing the cultural trends that create the environment in which congregations minister today. In the same way that a preacher or Bible study leader exegetes the biblical text by examining the historical background, the use of specific words, the main ideas, and the underlying presuppositions, so congregational leaders need to pay attention to the trends that are shaping the culture we live in and serve. The word "worldview" is also commonly used in this discussion to describe the presuppositions and values that shape the way people understand their lives. Exegeting culture, or teasing out the unstated worldview from entertainment media and advertising, requires paying attention to both spoken words and many forms of unspoken communication, including visual images, music, and body language.

Paul Windsor, who teaches preaching throughout Southeast Asia for Langham Partnership, advocates exploring the worldview presented in movies, television shows, novels, video games, songs, and other forms of story-telling and entertainment. He loves to lead groups of Christians into discussion by choosing one current movie, television show, video game, popular song, advertisement, or other cultural artifact. He places four empty chairs in the room and gives each of the chairs a label:

- the good
- the bad
- the new
- the perfect

He asks participants to analyze the bit of popular culture he has chosen. What is it saying about each of the four categories? What would this movie, show, or song put in each of the four chairs?[4]

About fifteen years ago when I was a pastor in a congregation, I remember coming away from a particular movie realizing that the filmmakers were subtly saying that sexual freedom was the ultimate good, the most powerful way humans can experience the freedom to be themselves. I didn't have Paul Windsor's four categories in mind at the time, but as I look back I can see the way my reflection on the worldview of that movie fit into his categories. For those moviemakers, "the good" was sexual freedom, and "the bad" was sexual repression. "The new" was a call to move beyond old-fashioned concepts like fidelity in marriage and self-restraint in sexual matters, and "the perfect" was a society where there were no limits at all for sexual expression.

Karl Barth argues that the Bible has to have priority as we study both the Bible and the newspaper. John Stott argues that we study the Bible in order to obey God, while we study the culture in order to sympathize with the needs of people, and in order to "to seek grace to discover how the gospel relates to it."[5] As I pondered that movie, and the view of sexuality promoted by that movie, I wondered what grace looks like in a culture influenced by that view. I wondered how the Gospel speaks into that view. I found myself pondering my ministry in a congregation where people are influenced by movies, television shows, and novels with that worldview. I found myself thinking about my sermons, the adult classes I taught, and my pastoral counseling appointments.

Two books give somewhat different, but equally helpful, frameworks for exegeting culture. In *The Transforming Vision*, University of Toronto chaplain Brian Walsh and Northeastern Seminary professor Richard Middleton lay out four questions that get at the issues related to worldview:

- Who are we? (What is the nature, task, and purpose of human beings?)
- Where are we? (What is the nature of the world and the universe in which we live?)
- What's wrong? (What is the basic obstacle that keeps us from attaining fulfillment?)
- What is the solution? (How is it possible to overcome this hindrance?)[6]

In *Earthcurrents*, Asbury Seminary professor Howard Snyder sets out another list. He argues that a worldview answers life's ultimate questions about:

- purpose (Is there a purpose to life? If so, what is it?)
- design (What is the design of the universe?)
- relationships (How does my life relate to other people, to history, and to the universe?)
- the future (Where is history going? Is there an end, or goal, to history?)[7]

Any of the three frameworks described here can be used to listen to the wider culture for the purpose of teasing out the values and priorities that underlie so many of forms of entertainment. A parish council, a small group meeting in a home, an adult class at church, or a book group can analyze a movie, television show, novel, video game, advertisement or popular song using one or more of the three lists here. The discussion can begin with an exploration of the worldview or worldviews presented, then move on to the question of how the Gospel speaks to that worldview, and ultimately come to the question of how this specific congregation is being given grace by God to make a difference in some way connected to the worldview being discussed.

These three ways of looking at worldview can also be used in congregational discussions to analyze the ethos of the congregation itself. In this congregation, what do we consider to be the good, the bad, the new, and the perfect? In this congregation, what do our sermons, printed materials, budget, activities, and casual conversations reveal about who are we, where are we, what's wrong, and what the solution is? A friend of mine, who has been serving a congregation for a couple of years, recently told me that he has been listening to the ethos of his congregation. He has seen some aspects of that ethos that concern him, and those concerns are shaping his sermons and his prayers. Analyzing worldview, then, can help individuals or groups get in touch with values and priorities in congregations or other organizations, as well as the ideals promoted by contemporary culture.

LISTENING TO GOD

In this chapter on listening to the unspoken, a brief discussion about listening to God is appropriate, even though that topic will be addressed more deeply later, in chapters 5 through 7. When my interviewees talked about listening to God, they described patterns that included verbal and nonverbal communication, as well as spoken and unspoken communication. My interviewees talked about hearing God speak to them through sermons, personal and small group Bible study, the words of friends, the beauty and power of nature, church architecture, and quiet inner nudges. Some people described hearing God's voice as they journaled or reflected on the pattern of their lives.

I have experienced God's clear guidance several times while walking a labyrinth. One time, in my last year as an associate pastor in a Presbyterian congregation in Seattle, I had been experiencing nudges for several months that made me think the time was coming when I would need to leave the congregation and do something else. I was resisting those nudges with everything in me. I loved the congregation and had planned to stay there until retirement. My husband and I took a vacation to San Francisco, and I walked the outdoor labyrinth at Grace Cathedral with its beautiful view of the city. During those moments walking that ancient pattern, I relinquished my future into God's hands and received a strong sense of peace about leaving the church I had been serving. I also felt a certainty that I would be leaving it fairly soon.

Three weeks later an unexpected event happened that reinforced my certainty that I would need to leave the congregation soon. A few weeks after that, I read an article in *Christian Century* that talked about the need in seminaries for people with experience in ministry, plus a Ph.D., to teach practical ministry courses. I read the article one evening, set it aside, then felt compelled to read it again an hour later. Again I set it aside, and an hour later picked it up and read it a third time. The words on those pages called to me. So I immediately began looking into Ph.D. programs in my city, and within a few months I was enrolled in one. Three years after that, I got my first teaching position. The shift from pastoral ministry to teaching has been wonderful in almost every way and exactly right for me.

That moment when I walked the labyrinth at Grace Cathedral and experienced God's peace about leaving the church I loved illustrates several issues pertinent to this chapter on unspoken communication. Sometimes our bodies—as we walk, kneel, garden, or do some other physical activity—open the ears of our heart to hear God's voice or the Holy Spirit's nudges. Sometimes God's voice comes to us in nonverbal ways, such as through a sense of peace about a decision or a certainty that something new is coming in our life. My intense reaction to that *Christian Century* article illustrates the fact that sometimes written words speak to us powerfully, and the drive I experienced to pick up the article several times in the same evening was probably part of God's guidance to me.

Our congregations are filled with people who are experiencing or who have experienced God's nudging, God's clear guidance, and a sense of God's peace in the midst of confusing times. Making a place to talk about those experiences helps normalize them and encourages members to keep listening for God's voice to them. Congregational leaders who desire to move beyond a management style of church governance need to figure out ways to talk about and nurture a sense that God guides individuals and groups within the congregation in big and small decisions.

LISTENING TO CREATION

Psalm 19 affirms that the physical world speaks without words:

> The heavens are telling the glory of God;
> and the firmament proclaims his handiwork.
> Day to day pours forth speech,
> and night to night declares knowledge.
> There is no speech, nor are there words; their voice is not heard;
> yet their voice goes out through all the earth,
> and their words to the end of the world. (verses 1–4)

The psalmist understands the theme of this chapter, that we often "hear" speech that does not involve words or even sounds.

The psalmist argues that creation speaks to us in many ways. As more congregations are participating in caring for the earth as a manifestation of their faith commitment, the perspective of Psalm 19 takes on increased significance. In what ways is the creation speaking to us today? In what ways can congregations listen more carefully? Psalm 19 makes clear that the voice of creation calls us to worship. I majored in biology as an undergraduate, and I worshipped God as deeply in the biology lab as I did in the student Christian fellowship group. Bacteria and algae under a microscope spoke to me of God's order and attention to detail, and I felt awe. The complexity of physiological systems spoke to me of God's ability to create intricate, interconnected structures. Outdoors, the colors of nature—in leaves, flowers, birds, and tropical fish—spoke to me of God's beauty.

Mountains, skies, seas, rivers, lakes, trees, and flowers continue to speak to me of God's beauty and infinite majesty, and I continue to respond by praising the God who made them and who speaks to me through them. However, the pollution of the earth speaks to me as well. The plastic in the ocean that kills beautiful seabirds makes me ache. The chemicals in food and air that have infiltrated human and animal bodies make me grieve. The rising carbon and methane in the atmosphere that is causing damage to human life for the most vulnerable make me mourn. Creation speaks in ways that transcend words and calls us to respond. What is creation saying? Pondering the way creation speaks can help nurture a congregation's commitment to caring for creation. In addition, the voice of creation can help us remember the many forms of communication that do not involve spoken words.

DOES UNSPOKEN COMMUNICATION BLOCK LISTENING?

Unspoken communication in diverse forms surrounds us. In many settings, it bombards us, and we spend a fair amount of our daily lives responding to it. Is it blocking the kinds of listening that undergirds relationships? A recent article in our local newspaper described some new research indicating that people under the age of thirty experience significantly more loneliness than people between the ages of thirty and sixty-four. One of the experts interviewed for the article suggested that social media might have increased the expectations of connectedness among people under thirty. Another interviewee for the article suggested that smart phones have allowed people to be online even more, increasing connections with people not present but decreasing face-to-face connection.[8]

Fifteen, and ten, and even five years ago I was quite skeptical about the many voices saying electronic communication is dangerous. I loved email from the moment I first tried it, and I have had many deep and meaningful email exchanges with friends. I enjoy Facebook as a way to nurture connections with old friends or distant friends and to discover interesting things to read through the links people post. I find blogs to be a fascinating window into the thoughts of friends, colleagues, acquaintances, and strangers. I studied church websites for my Ph.D., and I am often incredibly grateful for the information available on the myriad websites created by organizations and individuals. For congregations, electronic communication presents many opportunities to share resources and to disseminate information about activities and priorities. In addition, websites, blogs, Facebook, and other forms of online communication offer great opportunities to gather information about the world we live in and about people and their concerns.

In spite of my early enthusiasm about the online world, in the past few years I have found myself increasingly concerned about the effect of electronic communication on human relationships. I think the tipping point for me has come from the proliferation of smart phones. Increasingly I read newspaper and magazine articles citing research that indicates electronic communication may be having unintended consequences. I've been asking young adults I know if they think people their age find it hard to be present in face-to-face conversations, and many of them say yes. It's just too easy, they say, to put in your ear buds and listen to music when you feel uneasy in public. It's too easy to text someone with your cell phone or surf the web when you feel uncomfortable in a social situation. It's too easy to spend hours online rather than talk to your housemates or family members. And now that the Internet is available wherever you go, all of these challenges are compounded. If you didn't have electronic options, young adults have told me, you might persevere in trying to relate to the person next to you.

What can congregations do in response? Online and cell phone communication is not going away, but we can encourage limits to their use while affirming the opportunities they present. One idea is to encourage occasional technology fasts, where the cell phone or smart phone is put away for a day, a weekend, or even longer. This year, several of my Facebook friends announced at the beginning of Lent that they were going to fast from Facebook during Lent. Any specific technology can be the target of a fast: computers, tablets, smart phones, email, surfing the web, iPods, and so on. Fasting opens up time, and that time can be used for Bible study and prayer. That time can also be used for conversations with people who are present. Whole congregations or small groups can fast together, which provides opportunities to support each other in the fast, pray together about what's being learned, and debrief together afterward.

Another idea is to talk about technology and the Sabbath, encouraging people to think about putting aside electronic connections—or at least some of them—one day a week in order to nurture face-to-face connections, enjoyment of nature, and a quieter pace. The Sabbath is a day to stop working. How much of our electronic communication feels like work? The Sabbath is a day to step back from the stress of daily life, and some Sabbath keepers have told me they try to avoid the stress of multitasking on the Sabbath. Setting aside a tablet or smart phone for a day can decrease multitasking.

Small groups and committees can brainstorm about how to cope with cell phones during gatherings and meetings. I recently heard about a group of friends who, when they gather for a meal, put all their phones in the middle of the table, set to vibrate. When one phone vibrates, it disturbs the whole pile, and the person whose phone vibrates first has to pay more for their share of the meal than everyone else. And if someone grabs their phone from the pile to look at the screen, that person has to pay an even greater share.

Electronic communication appears to be having an isolating effect on people, and any sermon or class on listening needs to creatively address this challenge. A brainstorming session about how to cope with cell phones during a meeting or meal might help participants think creatively about this big challenge. Encouragement to fast from technology, and to find some partners to do it with, might help participants increase in their ability to listen to others and to God. Electronic communication is evidently here to stay, but we need to evaluate the ways it makes listening possible and the ways it impedes listening.

THE VALUE OF FOCUSING ON THE UNSPOKEN

Unspoken communication can give us so much information, and it can also be so confusing and distracting. I love to see the smile of a friend, and yet when I see a gesture by someone from another culture, I often don't know what it means. I think I'll be growing all the rest of my life in my ability to attend carefully to unspoken communication.

We depend on our eyes so much in communication, and we need our ears not just to hear words but also to perceive a wide variety of other sounds that convey meaning. Sometimes I think about what it would be like to be deaf or blind. What would I miss the most? In what ways would my relationships be changed? How would I compensate? Sometimes I think about Helen Keller, who was both deaf and blind, and I think about that moment of revelation when Helen realized her teacher was using Helen's hand to create symbols that represent words. We were made to connect with others in a variety of ways, and even Helen Keller, without the ability to hear or see, developed the skill to do that.

The remainder of this book focuses mostly on listening to spoken speech, but many forms of unspoken communication have great significance as well. We connect with others in so many ways that do not involve listening to words, and congregations today are "speaking" in many ways that do not involve sounds, through their buildings, grounds, newsletters, websites, social networking, and the visual arts. Congregational leaders are paying attention to unspoken communication by studying demographic trends, observing cultural values and worldviews in entertainment media, reading local newspapers and many kinds of online material, and listening to nature. We experience God's guidance and presence in many ways that are beyond words and sounds, and that communication enriches relationships within families, congregations, and the wider community.

QUESTIONS FOR REFLECTION, JOURNALING, AND GROUP DISCUSSION

- Spend some time thinking about the place of unspoken communication in your life. Where do you "hear" it most often—online, through reading, through cell phone texting, elsewhere? What role has unspoken communication played in your life, and what do you think about its significance?
- In what ways do visual art and visual images speak to you? What do they say? Where do you hear their voices most often? In what ways does or could your congregation "listen" and "speak" using visual arts and visual communication?
- Have you ever seen a movie or television show, listened to a popular song, or read a novel that revealed to you something about the worldview of the people who created it? What worldview or worldviews were evident? Of the three frameworks given in this chapter for "exegeting culture," which one seems most helpful to you?
- Think about your strengths and weaknesses at listening to things unspoken. Write a prayer asking for God's help to grow in this area.
- Do you know someone who seems quite aware of the worldview presented in movies, television shows, movies, popular songs, and advertisements? Or do you perhaps know someone who is particularly attuned to the way creation speaks? Pay a compliment to that person, and ask what has enabled that kind of listening.

3

LISTENING WITHIN THE CONGREGATION

It is a listening skill to acknowledge the person who is talking.

It is a listening skill to help keep the conversation going.

It is a listening skill to show some approval of the other person and what they are saying.

It is a listening skill to be able to feed back to the other person what they said and intended rather than what you selected from what they said.

—Richard Dimbelby and Graeme Burton, *More Than Words: An Introduction to Communication*[1]

At the end of choir practice, Will and Tom found themselves walking to the parking lot together. "How are you doing?" Will asked. "Last time we talked, you thought your supervisor might be transferred to another position, and you were wondering if there was any chance you'd be considered for the supervisor job. What happened with that?"

"It's still up in the air," Tom responded. "I'm trying to be patient, but it's hard!" Both men laughed, and Tom continued. "I'm quite concerned about two people on my team who are having a lot of trouble with the uncertainty. I've been trying to figure out how I can help them feel more secure." The two men continued to talk for a few more minutes about Tom's job, then Tom asked about Will's teenage son, Jason, who had been caught shoplifting a few months earlier.

Will responded by describing the court-ordered diversion process, which involved community service. "Jason is alternately grateful that he didn't get a conviction on his record and sullen about that fact that so many of his friends shoplift and don't get caught. I'm trying to be grateful to God that Jason was caught, because in my best moments I really do believe that the whole process will teach him something." While the summer sky darkened and other choir members got into their cars to drive home, Will and Tom stood beside Tom's car for twenty minutes, talking about these situations. When the conversation ended, they promised to pray for each other.

The following Sunday, Will's wife, Joleen, helped clean up the kitchen after coffee hour. Working alongside her were Nancy and Simon, parents of a teenage daughter who had recently started criticizing her parents. "I don't know which is worse," Joleen said as she put cups in the dishwasher, "the critical words you get from your daughter, or the silence I get from Jason when I try to talk with him about the community service he's doing. It was so much easier when they were little, even though it didn't feel easy at the time. I don't know how to pray for teenagers."

"You know," Nancy said, "I've been praying for years that when my kids do something wrong, they would get consequences that would teach them something important. I also pray that they wouldn't suffer serious harm from those consequences. It seems to me that's exactly what happened with Jason. He got caught, there were consequences, but they're not on his permanent record, so he wasn't harmed. I guess God answered my prayer, only it was your son, not mine, who got the answer."

"Hmmm, that's an interesting prayer," Joleen replied. "And helpful."

CONGREGATIONAL CONVERSATIONS MATTER

Serious conversations, and the listening that makes them possible, take place in numerous settings in congregations. Conversations in some settings are informal and unplanned, such as in kitchens after coffee hour and parking lots after choir practice. Some congregational settings are designed for conversation: small groups, board meetings, committees, retreats, men's and women's gatherings, coffee hour, and congregational meals. Boards and committees need to listen carefully as they make decisions, and chapter 5 focuses on the role of listening in decision making.

All conversations in congregations require a listener who pays attention to the person speaking, and recent research by sociology of religion professor Nancy Ammerman reveals the importance of such conversations. Ammerman and her team interviewed a large number of American adults about their spiritual lives. The interviewees all came from a Judeo-Christian background, and their current religious convictions ranged from atheism to deep commitment to Christianity or other forms of spirituality or religion. The goal of the research was to listen to stories about people's lives in order to see how religion and spirituality play a role.[2]

Ammerman found that the people who had the deepest spiritual commitments—whether to a Buddhist meditation practice or the Christian faith—frequently talked with others about the spiritual dimensions of everyday life. Ammerman described the content of these conversations as the overlap of "the ordinary and the nonordinary" or the intersection of the "sacred and the secular." These conversations allow the conversation partners to explore divine action in human life, to encounter faith in everyday life, or to talk about "something that calls us beyond ourselves." According to Ammerman's research, these conversations take place most often in homes, workplaces, and communities of faith. In fact, she argues that communities of faith play a significant role in helping individuals learn to "speak" religion. Congregational settings where conversations take place allow individuals to express connections between the sacred and ordinary events of their lives. And the stories they hear others tell in congregational settings enable them to consider new ways faith might spill over into everyday life.

As they stood beside Tom's car on a summer night, both Will and Tom asked questions to draw out the other. Both men received the gift of a listening ear, and each got to express his thoughts and feelings because the other listened. In addition to being able to talk, Will got to hear Tom express his concern for the vulnerable members of his team, which might encourage Tom to look out for vulnerable people in his own workplace. At one point in the conversation, Tom alluded to the fact that his concern for his team came directly from his faith commitment. Tom received the gift of a conversation in which to make that connection, and Will got to listen to Tom talk about it, so both men benefitted. At the end of the conversation, Will and Tom agreed to pray for each other. Even that seemingly small commitment affirms the spiritual significance of the challenges they had been discussing and exemplifies the overlap between the sacred and the secular.

While washing dishes, Joleen, Nancy, and Simon got to think out loud about the relevance of their faith in parenting teenagers. Joleen got to hear Nancy talk about one way Nancy has prayed for her children, which might encourage Joleen to pray in new ways. These conversations, Ammerman would argue, help the conversation partners in many ways. These conversations encourage reflection on the values and practices of the faith the individuals hold, and help the individuals act more congruently with their beliefs. In addition, the conversation partners become more comfortable talking about the intersection of their faith and their daily lives. This comfort in talking about the ways faith impacts daily life is then carried over into other settings such as the workplace, the home, and sometimes the neighborhood, where people also find spiritual conversation partners, and the conversation continues.

Ammerman noted that the people who find the time and energy to take part in various forms of mission outside congregations are those who are confident in their ability to talk about the overlap between everyday life and the sacred. They have experienced the impact of their faith in their daily lives, and they have gained the language and skills to talk about it. They are able to see that many components of their lives have a spiritual dimension, and they carry that conversation with them. In that sense, then, congregations are training grounds for mission, because they help members learn the skill of talking about the overlap of the ordinary and the nonordinary, the intersections of the sacred and the secular.

Conversations in congregations help us become comfortable listening to others talk about that overlap as well. For Christians, these conversations help us grow in recognizing God as an actor in our lives, Jesus as a companion, and the Holy Spirit as a guide and comfort, both because we say words out loud about those realities and because we listen to others talk about them. Speaking about this overlap and listening to others talk about it helps us see the fruits of a life that responds to God's presence with us. These perspectives and skills are essential for mission and ministry.

Ammerman's research indicates that a congregation's ability to create spaces for this kind of conversation is not correlated in any way with doctrine. Instead, the determining factor is individuals' participation in congregational activities. Congregations that encourage a wide variety of activities where people can participate in diverse ways create spaces for conversations, and those conversations "fuel up" individuals in a way that makes mission possible. In the address where I heard Ammerman speak, she reflected on the significance of patterns of congregational life: "We have said that what happens in congregations doesn't matter, but it does matter a lot."

Listening is essential in encouraging these deep conversations. Listening draws people out, giving them an opportunity to try out their stories. Listening skills elicit descriptions of where the sacred and the secular weave together. Growing in listening skills in a congregational setting can help us and others learn to be better "spiritual conversation partners" or "spiritual compatriots," which Ammerman views as a key building block for faith commitment and for mission.

SMALL GROUPS

One of the places in congregations where listening happens is the small group. In the first fifteen years of our marriage, my husband and I participated in small groups together as a couple. At that time, Dave was teaching in a dental school. As Dave's faith deepened over those years, his concern for dental ethics grew as well. I can remember countless small group sessions where he talked about his concern that the structure of the dental school lab sessions encouraged students to think of patients as a means to an end, because students had to find patients who needed specific procedures, either from among the patients who walked into the dental school clinics or by their own recruiting. He was concerned that viewing patients this way in dental school would carry over into dental practice. I tried to listen to Dave talk about this objectification of patients, and I hope I succeeded to some extent, but the others in our small groups listened in ways that went far beyond my abilities.

One of our small groups lasted several years. A woman in that group was working on a graduate degree at the same university where Dave was teaching, and she expressed her own frustrations with the university structures in a way that encouraged Dave to continue to explore his concerns. Another woman worked as a lab technician in a hospital, and she was able to relate to Dave's concerns because of the medical issues raised by her job. Her husband was a businessman, and his job provided further connections between business ethics, dental offices, and the Christian faith. Dave received support from the group members as he talked through his concerns and tried to figure out the best response. The support took two forms: they listened to him as he thought out loud, and the stories of their own challenges provided examples of possible responses. That small group played a big role in his ability to work through the overlaps between his Christian faith and the ethical challenges of his job.

Janette, an Anglican who leads a home group with her husband, reflected on the way conversations in her group have equipped members to speak up about their faith and about ethics in workplaces and neighborhoods. She believes home groups encourage people to bring their faith into their everyday lives. She described her group:

> We study the Bible and pray for each other. The prayer requests are a mixture of family concerns and how can I be a Christian in my world. It's not possible to study the Bible and not get a concern for people around you. A home group is where people can say, "I want to have more of those conversations where I share my faith with people, but I'm a bit reluctant and apprehensive, in case I get it wrong."

The members of Janette's group often meet up for coffee after church in a café near the church. They like to analyze the sermon together, and they tend to catch up with what's been happening in each other's lives, following up on some of the prayer requests from the previous group meeting.

Janette is a member of a large congregation with many home groups. She believes that "in order to thrive as a big church, you need strong nurturing home groups." When I interviewed Janette, her church was about to have a celebration dinner for house group leaders, and she described the many ways small group leaders are supported in her church. House groups are divided into pastorates, which include three or four groups, and a church lay leader provides oversight and support for the leaders of those groups. The support includes inviting the leaders to supper on a regular basis and praying for them. Some of Janette's enthusiasm for leading a small group comes from the fact that "it's so wonderful to be looked after." Janette's ability to listen to the cares and concerns in her group comes in part from the support and listening she receives.

One of my interviews was with a group, the minister of an urban congregation and five other members of that congregation, all of them board members or lay leaders. Several of them attend a small group that meets weekly to talk about the lectionary passages that were used in the sermon the previous week. One of them said about that group, "Our purpose is to listen to the lectionary and respond to the sermon. The text becomes really rich. People take the time to listen to each other, but also to ask questions about what we see in the passage." Another person chimed in, "And we pray for each other."

The minister described a new pattern for the board meetings. The session had begun meeting twice a month, once for business and once for a potluck dinner and conversation "where we listen to each other and grow together. We've managed to stumble on a safe place for people to be real." Another person described a men's group he attends at church as one more "safe place" within the congregation, where members have a diversity of theological opinions that they feel free to express because the group listens well. The minister responded, "People need to be heard, and that's an end in itself."

His comment precipitated a fascinating discussion about the purpose of listening. One woman said, "Merely being present to another human is a ministry." She used the phrase "ministry of presence" to describe a combination of listening, praying, and following up that indicates to the conversation partner that the listener is genuinely paying attention. One of the men observed that listening usually has a purpose, and often the listener has an agenda in listening, such as getting information or persuading the other person about a certain point of view. Another woman replied, "Sometimes people just need to be heard. They need to talk." She recommended using all five senses when listening.

The group went back and forth about the value of simply being present to another person and letting that person guide the direction of the conversation, rather than listening with a specific purpose in mind. Small groups in congregations involve both kinds of conversations. Sometimes simply listening to a person's viewpoints or concerns is the most important thing to do, and other times participants argue for their perspective on the Bible passage or the book, video, or issue being discussed. In both kinds of conversation, both the speakers and the listeners can grow in their ability to make connections between their faith commitments and their everyday lives.

Small groups can get short-circuited by people who dominate. Jane, a minister and theological college lecturer, said, "Leaders need to know how to shut people up. In a small group or meeting, if someone is dominating, either by dismissing people's ideas or trying to impose their own, the leader needs to know how to quiet that voice without silencing it completely." Jane advocated that the leader's role include helping participants be open to difference, because interacting with a variety of understandings is creative and positive. She believes that the goal of small group discussions should not be to aim at uniformity. Grappling with diverse views can happen "by engaging with the Bible, because, for example, each of the Gospels tells a different story. The Bible has more than one voice, more than one way of understanding. Small groups need to engage with the variety of the ways the Bible tells things."

Small groups can also lose effectiveness when the leader has a strong agenda. An Anglican woman mentioned two kinds of groups in her congregation. Several of them are led by the minister, and she noted, "He has an agenda of what he wants to cover. It's not a discussion group; it's a very guided discussion on a topic. Most people speak to the minister rather than to each other." She also mentioned an informal dinner group in her congregation that had been together for many years, where the members provided a great deal of support to each other.

In my interviews I heard about small groups that include Bible study, discussion of a book or video, sharing personal stories and praying for each other, talking informally and providing support, various forms of silent prayer or contemplation, and many combinations of these components. According to my interviewees, what makes a group successful is that the members are able to talk honestly about their faith and their lives in the presence of people who genuinely listen. Nancy Ammerman's research echoes the perspective of my interviewees. Small groups in congregations provide a significant place for people to grow in their ability to figure out and articulate the intersection of their faith and their everyday lives.

PASTORAL CARE LISTENING

Pastoral care involves giving emotional and spiritual support, and congregations have often stressed the role of listening in providing that support. Therefore, classes and seminars on listening in seminaries, church governing bodies, and congregations have often focused on pastoral care. In the past, pastoral care was usually viewed primarily as the province of ministers and chaplains, but recently more congregations are establishing pastoral care teams of lay people. As described above, small groups function as places of pastoral care, because emotional and spiritual support plays such a big role in small groups. I believe every person of faith is called to provide pastoral care at times, because all of us can give emotional and spiritual support in at least some situations. And I believe listening skills play a major role in providing that support.

Emotional and spiritual support takes many forms. I had a major surgery last year. While I was in the hospital, several friends and family members sent me flowers, and I felt so loved and supported. After I got home, several friends brought meals, and I felt loved and supported again. Several other friends came to visit in my first couple of weeks home, and again I was so grateful that they cared enough to come. I got several cards, too, that expressed caring and concern. In the midst of all that love and support, however, I noticed that listening was pretty thin on the ground, and I longed for people with whom I could talk through the variety of feelings I was experiencing.

My husband was busy taking care of me after I got home from the hospital, and I didn't want to burden him with my tumultuous emotions. What did I wish I could have talked about with visitors? I spent five days in the hospital after the surgery. I had been in the hospital only twice before, when my two sons were born. My sons are now adults, so those two hospital stays were long, long ago. My days in the hospital this time were full of confusing events, including an argument with my anesthesiologist about the vitamins I had brought with me and night sweats that required summoning a nurse numerous times for a total change of bedding. The five days seemed to last several weeks and were full of upheaval, and even weeks afterward I was still processing how I felt about those days. In addition, I was quite afraid about the recovery period. I was trying to be optimistic, but fears kept creeping in, and I would have liked to have had a listening ear so I could talk my way through my anxiety.

In the conversations I had in the first weeks after the surgery, I noticed a pattern. The visitor would ask me how I was feeling, and I would talk for a while, maybe the equivalent of several paragraphs. I would then ask my visitor how he or she was doing, and we would move into a general conversation. I had many more thoughts swirling around inside me that I would like to have talked about, but I didn't want to keep talking about them unless asked. And most visitors, once I switched the topic, did not return to the topic of my surgery. Perhaps they felt they didn't want to intrude.

Recently a friend of mine had an emergency surgery. On her second day home from the hospital, I phoned her. I asked if she had the time and energy to talk, and she said yes. So I asked her about the lead-up to the surgery. How did she decide to go to the emergency room? What happened there? What tests did they give her? I tried to keep her talking for a while by using those small sounds called minimal encouragers that indicate we are listening: "hmmm" and "wow." I tried to reflect back on what I heard, using brief phrases to keep her talking: "an ultrasound" and "your husband stayed with you."

After she had talked for five or ten minutes about the lead-up to the surgery, she changed the subject and asked me how I was doing. I answered her briefly, but based on my experience with my surgery, I knew there were two other big topics that we hadn't talked about—her hospital stay and her thoughts and fears about recovery—so next I asked about her time in the hospital. I tried to give her ample time to talk about her hospital stay by again using minimal encouragers and reflection and by asking brief questions. Then we talked about some other topics. Later in the conversation I asked about her thoughts and fears about her recovery.

This kind of focused listening matters for at least two reasons. On the one hand, letting people talk as long as they want to about a traumatic or happy event communicates that we care enough to want to hear about whatever they have to say about it and that we are willing to serve them by letting them process their thoughts and feelings out loud. If "providing emotional and spiritual support" is the key component of pastoral care, then letting people talk about their experiences is a form of support. In addition, letting people talk at length about significant life events gives them time to work their way around to reflecting on where they experienced God's presence. In other words, we allow them to have enough time and space to articulate, in Nancy Ammerman's words, the overlap of the sacred and the sacred, or the intersection of the everyday and the extraordinary.

In the case of my friend who had just had emergency surgery, when I asked her about her hospital stay, she said she was so grateful that her sister-in-law had worked for many years on the ward where she stayed. Once the nurses found out that my friend was related to their former colleague, they gave her extra attention, and my friend saw that as a manifestation of God's care for her. If I hadn't moved the conversation to the topic of her hospital stay, she wouldn't have had the opportunity to talk about the way she experienced God's care there. Toward the end of the conversation, after she had talked about her thoughts about her recovery, she circled back to the decision to go to the emergency room, and she said that she felt God's guidance in making that decision. Making space for enough listening time so my friend could get to the topic of God's presence in the situation is a gift that I was determined to give her, and I tried to express to her my joy that she experienced God's guidance and care in the midst of this medical emergency.

All traumatic events have a lead-up, a central event or events, and a recovery time. In conversations focused on medical issues, a death, a natural disaster, a job loss, or any other kind of crisis, a listener can focus a series of questions on those three periods, allowing the conversation partner enough time to talk at length about each of the three. Most happy events—such as weddings, births, and new jobs—also have a lead-up, a central event or events, and the time afterward, and happy events can also be a topic of pastoral care listening. As happened with my friend, the conversation might shift to something else for a while, which reduces the intensity for a few minutes. The listener can then later return the conversation to the major event by asking a question that moves the conversation to a time related to the event that hasn't been discussed yet. The listener might say something like, "You talked about the events leading up to your job loss, but I haven't heard about what happened after you got that news."

If given enough time, people will often get to their thoughts and feelings about God's presence with them in the trauma or happy event. If they don't get there, I try to open the door to that topic by saying something like, "I'm hoping you experienced God's comfort in the midst of it" or "I've been praying for a sense of Jesus walking with you in this." People often do have a sense of God's presence in small moments in times of trauma, even if they also have big questions and concerns about what happened. Sometimes the speaker's central spiritual experience in trauma is the absence of God. A listener can give the gift of letting the person process those feelings out loud. However, fears about how to respond to those feelings often shut down the listening process, because we as listeners are afraid that we will have to produce answers. Chapter 9 discusses the ways listeners can cope with such anxiety that arises during listening. With most people in trauma, however, I've observed a mix of questions about God's absence, coupled with a sense of God's presence in small or big ways. Giving people the opportunity to talk about both is a gift.

Catherine, a Presbyterian minister who trained as a chaplain, talked about the significance of prayer as a part of pastoral care conversations. She said that in chaplaincy training,

> I'd sit with people, listen to their stories, then offer to pray for them. In the prayer, I would try to bring the depth of the conversation to God. Ninety-five percent of the time they would share something much deeper after the prayer, often with tears in their eyes. The heart of the issue was often something else, and they were willing to express it after the prayer.

Often, the "heart of the issue" is that sense of where God is present in the significant events the person has recently experienced.

Some people simply don't want to talk about what they have experienced, or they don't want to talk at length about it. That makes minimal encouragers and reflecting so important in pastoral care listening, because they give the speaker the option not to continue. Perhaps I'm listening to someone talk about the stress of finding out their child has a learning disability, and I say "hmmm" to try to indicate that I'm willing to listen longer, but the person chooses not to say more. I need to be willing to let the speaker set the pace for the conversation, and I need to refrain from jumping in with a series of direct questions to attempt to keep the conversation going.

A few days after the conversation with my friend about her emergency surgery, I asked her by email if I could tell the story of that conversation in this book. She said yes, and then she went on to write:

> I have the feeling that most often people do not want to hear the details of someone's sickness or traumatic event, perhaps because they are uncomfortable with medical details, they don't want a "downer," or they don't want their own past or present stories to be upstaged. And I know that I worry about being a complainer if I say too much about my own trials, so I look for the positive and try to minimize the details. I do think people need to talk about a hospital experience because it's such a unique time. You're so vulnerable. I think it is therapeutic for people to be able to talk about their traumatic experience in some way.

Pastoral care listening is often viewed as something quite separate from mission. One of my interviewees pointed out, however, that the most enthusiastic people in the Gospels, who talked about Jesus freely, were the ones who were healed by him. Because pastoral care listening can reduce the stress of trauma, and reducing stress usually contributes to healing, this kind of caring listening can indeed equip people for mission if the healing is perceived as coming from God's care. The connection between pastoral care listening and mission is illuminated by Nancy Ammerman's research, which indicates that the people who are most equipped for mission are those who have learned to articulate the overlap between their everyday lives and the sacred. Pastoral care listening provides one way for that to happen.

LISTENING IN OTHER CONGREGATIONAL SETTINGS

If pastoral care is defined as providing emotional and spiritual support, then many conversations in congregations have a component of pastoral care. Pastoral care happens in small groups, after worship services where someone is available to pray with people in need, and in places like hospitals where a minister or lay pastoral caregiver has come for the express purpose of listening, caring, and praying. However, pastoral care also happens in informal conversations at coffee hour, congregational meals, men's and women's events, retreats, before and after meetings, and in hallways and parking lots. Listening skills are essential for everyone in a congregation, because everyone at one time or another has the opportunity to provide pastoral care to people who have something significant on their minds.

Pastoral care listening helps the speaker articulate the connections between their faith and the situation they're describing, but listening in other kinds of conversations accomplishes that goal as well. Discussions about the Bible or contemporary issues in small groups and adult classes helps make those connections come alive. Discussion in board meetings, committees, and ministry teams can help participants see where their faith intersects with the situation at hand. Children, teenagers, and young adults can see connections between God and life that are invisible to older adults, and they often raise intriguing questions about those connections. Ammerman's research indicates the significance of providing a variety of

activities where people can connect with each other across the genera-
tions and sub-groups within any congregation.

Worship Services

Many aspects of worship contribute to a congregational climate that encourages deep conversations and careful listening. Jenny, a member of
the ministry team at a Methodist church, talked about the new worship
space that her congregation built a few years ago. While waiting for the
construction of the new church, worshippers met in the fellowship hall
and were seated in curved rows that formed a half circle round the po-
dium. This idea of a more open and circular seating arrangement was
carried over into the design of the new worship space. Jenny believes that
being able to see each other during worship has contributed to a deeper
sense of fellowship and belonging, which continues in deeper conversations after the worship service. Somehow the bond between people is
strengthened by eye contact during worship.

Components of worship services can support the significance of listening to each other. Some congregations ask people ahead of time to
present testimonies as a part of the service. Some congregations allow for
brief, unscripted testimonies during worship. One congregation I visited
had an open microphone after the sermon. The service leader encouraged
worshippers to say something they liked about the sermon, report on an
answered prayer, or describe a prayer request. In another congregation,
every Sunday before the closing hymn a few moments are allotted to
"What My Faith Means to Me," a time when anyone in the congregation
can get up and talk about something that happened to them that spoke to
them of God's presence. One member of that congregation believes
"What My Faith Means to Me" has provided a listening opportunity for
everyone, and another member said these informal stories have contributed to a sense that this congregation is a safe place to be real.

Several of my interviewees talked about their experiences with café
church, where worshippers sit around tables. Often a meal is involved, so
participants have the opportunity to talk to each other as they eat. In café
church, usually at some point in the service the leader suggests a topic for
worshippers to discuss around their tables.

One of my interviewees was a staff member with a café church, and
she said that the conversations around the tables provided an excellent

opportunity for leaders "to watch for what people responded to and what grew them, what helped our congregation move and develop."

The Arts

Salina, a church staff member, talked about a church she used to attend that often had an artist in residence for a season. Salina described a photographer, a poet, and a musician who had each served in that role consecutively over the course of a year. The congregation had a Sunday evening service, often focused on the arts. In that service, the poet in residence presented poems as a part of the homily, or the musician performed. Worshippers were given time during the service to walk around the worship space and look at photos the photographer had installed. In all cases, the artists presented works that related to the lectionary readings. At one point in the worship service, the service leader shared a few thoughts about his or her experience of the poems, photographs, or music, and then invited the worshippers to say a few words about their own observations. The services were characterized by lots of silence and careful listening to the artists and to the people who spoke up. Salina said she particularly enjoyed observing the fruit of the artists' listening to the lectionary readings and the response of the community as they listened to the art and to each other during those Sunday evening services.

In chapter 2 I noted that the visual arts are a form of unspoken communication. With the rise in visual culture over recent decades, the visual arts are playing an increasingly significant role in communicating about religious and spiritual issues. In fact, more congregations are making room for many kinds of art, poetry, and music. All arts—visual, verbal, and musical—provide an opportunity for participants to listen to the voice of the artist, and all arts can provide a platform for participants to talk about what they have experienced. The arts can build bridges within a congregation and also with people in the wider community, and they can evoke fascinating observations about the overlap of faith and daily life.

Ministry in Daily Life

A Church of Scotland lay leader said, "We need to avoid the situation where people in congregations are serving in some way outside the congregation, and no one knows until they die and information about what they did is listed in their obituary or described in their funeral." An Anglican woman who is a spiritual director said that the leaders of her congregation have never validated her ministry in any way, nor have they publicly affirmed the ministries of a counselor or a retreat speaker in the congregation. Many church members have a sense of call to serve in community organizations. Congregational leaders need to listen to the lives and concerns of members and make a place for them to talk about what they do and how their faith intersects with their profession, ministry, or community service. One of my interviewees suggested:

> Ask your business people what countries they are buying from and selling to and pray publically for them and for those countries. Ask high school and college students which global issues they are studying—such as war and peace, AIDs, hunger, human trafficking, ecology, pollution, trade and economy—and pray publically for those issues.

Her suggestion would make possible many more connections between everyday life and faith values.

AN AGENDA AS WE LISTEN?

In one sense, all congregational listening needs to have an agenda or goal: helping people express the intersection of the secular and the sacred, the overlap between their everyday lives and their faith. In another sense, the goal of all congregational listening should be to grow in our ability to listen without an agenda. I talked about this issue with a group of three Presbyterian ministers. One of them said, "So much listening in congregations is done with an agenda. I want to listen without an agenda. Hopefully a pastor is one of the people who can listen and accept the person as they are. If we can listen without an agenda, we can affirm where God is in their midst." Another said, "There has to be space and silence and an open focus on the person. Where is God already speaking in the person's life? One person at least in a conversation has to hold that focus and openness." The third said, "The benefit of listening without an agenda is that there's a sense of relaxing because you don't have to formulate a response. That relaxing maybe opens you to that soul-to-soul connection." I love the vocabulary in these three statements, an emphasis on a "soul-to-soul connection," affirming "where God is in their midst," and where God is "already speaking into the person's life." These three ministers seem to believe that when we converse without an agenda, we are more likely to get to that central goal of providing a safe place for people to talk about where their faith intersects with their everyday life. One of them went on to talk about what's necessary inside herself in order to do that kind of listening: "In order for me to provide what's needed in a conversation, I need to continue to create boundaries and give myself silence and perspective. If I'm grounded and centered, what I offer to others will be better."

I talked with a writer who has led classes in his church to help people write about their life journey. He described the way his conversations have changed over the years:

> I used to ask questions to extract information. I treated quotes and responses as commodities to make one's story fit my expectations. Fortunately, I started to pay attention to how conversations benefited others. Good questions, combined with careful listening, can free others to reflect and explore their own questions—questions that can crack open a new awareness of their "unfinished story." Listening honors each person's journey. When people feel listened to, they invariably begin to unwrap their own journey, story by story.

Congregations have always been and continue to be significant venues where such conversations can happen.

QUESTIONS FOR REFLECTION, JOURNALING, AND GROUP DISCUSSION

- Spend some time pondering the patterns in your congregation. In what settings do you think the best listening happens, the kind of listening that allows people to talk about the overlap of their faith and their daily lives? In what settings do conversations tend to be superficial? What factors do you think contribute to the listening patterns you have observed?

- If you could do one thing to improve the listening patterns in your congregation, what would that one thing be? What factors would have to be addressed in order for that change to be made?
- What do you think are your strengths and weaknesses as a listener in your congregation? If you could do one thing differently as a listener when you talk to people in your community of faith, what would it be?
- Write a prayer for yourself as a listener in your congregation, asking for God's help to grow in the attitudes and skills that make for good listening. Continue the prayer, asking God for help with the listening patterns in the various settings in your congregation.
- This week, pay someone a compliment for the way he or she listens to others in your congregation. Ask where he or she learned to listen well.

4

LISTENING FOR MISSION

One of the primary tasks of the listener is to stay out of the other's way so the listener can discover how the speaker views his situation.
—Robert Bolton, "Listening Is More Than Hearing," in *Bridges Not Walls: A Book about Interpersonal Communication*[1]

The minister of an Anglican church in a suburb of a major city made a tentative agreement with a telephone company to install a cell phone tower in the spire of the church. The parish council members were surprised by the minister's unilateral tentative agreement and by his uncritical discussions with the telephone company, but in the midst of financial pressures the congregation was facing, the income promised by the telephone company would be very welcome. The parish council members began to discuss the pros and cons of the decision. Before they came to any conclusion, the news of the potential tower got out to the local community, which erupted into a furor. Demonstrators paced outside the church building, demanding that the church drop any plans to bring a cell phone tower into the neighborhood. The parish council was forced to listen to the congregation's neighbors in new ways. Unexpected events precipitated a listening process that no one anticipated.

This pattern of listening precipitated by an unexpected event is not uncommon. A fire gutted the building of a Methodist church located in a residential neighborhood, and the congregation's leaders found that people who lived in the neighborhood had opinions about what the replacement building should look like. The congregational leaders found themselves listening to the community more profoundly than ever before as they worked to define their priorities for a new building. These two examples demonstrate the opportunity presented by unexpected events, as well as a few of the challenges of listening to the wider community. In the case of the Methodist congregation, not all of their neighbors were happy with the design of the new church building. In the case of the Anglican congregation, the plans for the cell phone tower were dropped, so the congregation's leaders did respond to the community's point of view. But should a congregation always submit to everything the community wants? And what about situations in which the congregation is simply unable to meet the needs or desires of the community?

Our congregations are located in communities, regions, and countries that are influenced by worldwide entertainment, advertising, and news media. As described in chapter 2, congregational leaders need to pay attention to those influences. Congregations swim in a sea of values and priorities from national and global media, and in addition, they are situated in local communities with specific needs and concerns. Congregational leaders need to pay attention to the specifics of their neighborhoods and towns or cities. Sometimes an unexpected event will precipitate listening. Sometimes an intentional listening project is appropriate. At all times, a posture of listening can build relationships beyond the church into the wider community.

LISTENING LOCALLY AND INTENTIONALLY

In the first chapter of this book, I describe the way the members of Eileen's church listened to the concerns of the people who shopped at the church's sales to raise funds for overseas mission trips. In another congregation, located down the street from an elementary school, the parish council encouraged congregation members to listen to the needs of students and staff at the school, with the hopes of building more connections with the school. To the surprise of everyone at the church, the biggest need at the school was for help with head lice. A team of volunteers from the church began to comb students' hair and help parents in the battle against head lice. Several years have passed since this ministry began, and one of the elders at the church believes helping in this concrete way has done more than anything else to build strong relationships in their community. He commented:

We asked how we could help. This ministry has built credibility for the church. We're there to serve, not to tell them things. We're not seen as a threat, and we're not seen as fruit loops, because we went in to help without an agenda. We're welcome in the school, and they occasionally call on our community worker to check on families they're concerned about. We're viewed as a part of the community in a way we never were before.

Listening to the local community requires two commitments. The first is a willingness to take seriously the needs and concerns of the local community. The second is the readiness to establish a setting in the church community where perceptions about those needs and concerns can be discussed and prayed about, with the goal of responding appropriately. In many congregations, one or both of these commitments is lacking. In the Methodist church that had a fire and the Anglican church that considered erecting a cell phone tower, unexpected events forced the leaders of those congregations to make the commitment to listen to the community's concerns and to reflect together on what they heard.

Some congregations choose to set up structures for listening to their local community, even without a precipitating event. An illustration of intentional, focused, and thorough listening to the wider community comes from St. Stephen's Anglican Church, the parish church in a town in England of just under five thousand people. The two necessary commitments—the conviction that the needs of the local community matter and the creation of settings within the congregation to discuss, pray for, and respond to those needs—are very evident.

St. Stephen's is located in a town surrounded by farmland, making very clear where the "wider community" begins and ends. The town was originally served by several parish churches, but some years ago they joined into one team ministry based at St. Stephen's. Despite being an active congregation with frequent musical events and other parish activities, St. Stephen's connection to the town was limited. The parish council wanted to build opportunities for local mission, and they decided to set up a nine-month listening project to find out ways they could engage with and serve their town. The minister at St. Stephen's, Samuel, identified the purpose of the project as "trying to create a church that is useful to our village. That's what a mission-shaped church needs to be." Their listening centered around two basic questions: "What do you think of St. Stephen's? What do you want from your local church?"

The parish council asked those questions by different means in numerous settings. First, they sent out a questionnaire to every household in the town. Fourteen percent of the questionnaires were returned. Samuel, along with one parish council member, made himself available for conversations at pubs and school playgrounds at times that were advertised in the town newspaper. Samuel interviewed civic leaders, including teachers, the mayor, the president of the Rotary Club, and their Member of Parliament, asking their two central questions and always bringing along a parish council member to the interviews to provide a second set of ears. Members of the parish council also approached the bishop and archdeacon, asking what they saw to be unique about St. Stephen's. Every parish council member, committee chair, and congregational ministry leader was interviewed by Samuel plus one parish council member, and all the members of the congregation were invited to fill out a questionnaire. During the nine months of the listening project, the congregation adopted a new slogan: "Listening to God, listening to others." They used the slogan on their stationery and mentioned it in worship, hoping that the slogan might promote an attitude of receptivity to all the ideas flowing in from the listening project.

After the nine months of listening, a group of people were appointed to bring together all the information from the surveys and interviews. They drew up a ten-page summary. Samuel took that summary away for a month of retreat and then wrote a 10,000-word report for the parish council, trying to reflect what he heard. He also culled out ninety-five recommendations from the suggestions in the surveys and interviews, grouped into five "Marks of Mission." Samuel tried to be completely open and honest as he wrote his report and led discussions for parish council. "I told them up front everything I thought needed to change. I didn't have any aces up my sleeve, no secrets. They knew what I was thinking." The parish council met in a retreat setting to talk about the report and the ninety-five suggestions. Together they drew up an action plan of 1,500 words, a mission strategy for the next five years.

In the year after the listening project, fifty-five of the recommendations were acted on or begun, including revision of liturgies, employment of a full-time youth worker, a new children's program, an environmental policy, and a parish magazine. The congregation bought recording equipment, so local choirs and schools could use the church building and make recordings of their performances. Thus the church has become a resource for the whole region, not just their town. They also inaugurated a night club-style, drama-based church service once a month. The choir decided to sing only twice a month to free up slots on the worship schedule so new people could be involved in leading and performing music.

One recommendation involved changing worship times, including offering more mid-week services. Samuel pointed out that Sunday morning simply isn't the best time for many people to attend church. In the year before the listening project began, the average weekly attendance at worship services, mostly on Sunday, was 170 people. Two years after the listening project, the congregation had a total of seven to nine services each week, each offering a different worship style to address the needs of different groups of people, and the average weekly attendance at services had grown to 380, with much of the additional attendance occurring at mid-week services. Eight church members had been trained and licensed as authorized lay leaders, and the congregation had begun the process of hiring a second full-time priest.

Making the Listening Project Work

In reflecting on the nine months of listening, Samuel noted:

> We needed to listen, but the people in the village also needed to feel listened to. We worked hard at showing respect as we listened. Showing respect and enabling people to feel "listened to" requires time, lots of time. We tried to use nonverbals to communicate that we weren't in a hurry. We were prepared to let people speak to us when and where they wanted to—in a pub, at a school—coming to them rather than expecting them to come to us. We tried to give feedback during the listening process. Twice we wrote articles for the local newspaper to let the people in the town know what we were hearing and how we were responding.

Samuel mentioned several aspects of prayer and worship that he believes played a significant role in helping the project to go well. In one worship service, Samuel intentionally celebrated one thousand years of the church being there in that town, and he used that celebration to pitch the whole listening exercise as the continuation of God's work in that place. Once a month during the project, Samuel addressed the listening project in his sermon. He said, "In sermons, I have tried to develop a theology that God is already in the community. God is alive here in our village. God's footprints are all around us, and we need to watch for them, to listen for God in the voice of our community." In addition, the listening project was a major item of prayer during regularly scheduled prayer meetings and on Sundays in the worship service.

Samuel acknowledged that some church members expressed upset feelings and dissention throughout the process, but he worked very hard to keep the process open and honest to promote as much ownership as possible. As noted above, when Samuel talked with people in the town, he always brought along a parish council member, which assured that everything was heard by more than one person at St. Stephen's, and this increased the sense of ownership on the part of the parish council. Residents of the town also experienced some degree of ownership, because they felt heard by more than one person at the church. The articles in the local newspaper about the listening project also nurtured a sense of ownership by town residents. The response process within the congregation involved many of the parish council members, which increased their sense of ownership.

Samuel believes that if a congregation is going to enter into a time of intentional listening to the community,

> You can't do anything else as well. You can't unveil new projects. During that year, some people were very frustrated to have to wait and honor the process, even though some changes were obvious from the beginning. But it's about ownership, people buying in and seeing the purpose. It becomes a community vision.

Possibly the most striking comment Samuel made regarding the project came during a parish council meeting right before the planned start date. Samuel suggested they wait another month in order to pray some more about it. To encourage the parish council to wait, pray, and be sure they truly wanted to do this, he advised them: "When you've listened, you can't unhear what you've heard. Be sure you really want to listen and change."

LISTENING WHILE SERVING

St. Stephen's set out to listen to the community where the church is located, but not all such projects are as intentional. One of the most significant ministries for Iona Presbyterian Church, a North American urban congregation with about 500 in worship every Sunday, began with a "what if" comment. Over time, however, the ministry—a community meal—has grown and matured because of a lot of effective listening. That listening happened at the dinner itself, as bridges were built between people who would normally not encounter each other in daily life. A spirit of listening to each other and to God also characterized the church board meetings when issues related to the dinner were on the agenda, and that same spirit of listening infused the members of the dinner's leadership team.

The ministry began almost twenty years ago, when Iona built a new fellowship hall. Soon after the hall was built, a handful of Iona members were chatting on a Wednesday evening, standing near the glass doors at the front of the new building. Looking outside, the church members could see food bank patrons standing in line at the building next door, which housed the congregation's offices on the upper floor as well as an area food bank on the ground floor. One of the church members mused:

> What if we hosted a meal every Wednesday for the people who come to the food bank? And what if we encouraged people from the congregation to attend the meal as well, so it could become a place where people connect with each other, not just a place where we're giving something to people in need?

For more than a decade, Iona had been providing space for the food bank. Many Iona members, along with members of other neighborhood churches and people from the wider community, served as volunteers at the food bank. The Iona food bank volunteers enjoyed serving there, and they were grateful for the brief moments of contact with people from the community who needed food. But some of them longed for a setting where deeper relationships might develop and thought a weekly dinner might provide that opportunity. Food bank volunteers from other churches were enthusiastic about the idea, as were the church elders who were concerned that because Iona was an upper-middle-class church, the congregation had few connections to people from other socioeconomic groups.

From the beginning, the leaders of the dinner promoted it within the congregation as a place to build relationships. Elders and church staff were encouraged to make a regular commitment to come to the dinner, perhaps once a month, and simply eat and chat. Congregation members were encouraged to do the same. Volunteers were needed to cook and serve the meal, as well as clean up afterward, but all flyers and announcements asking for volunteers mentioned the option of simply attending the dinner for the purpose of talking and listening.

In the first few years of the dinner, about one-third of the people attending were patrons of the food bank. The dinner was served right after the food bank closed, so the food bank patrons often picked up their food and then came to the dinner. The homeless population of the city, not eligible for the food bank because they had no permanent address, learned about the free dinner, and they came in strong numbers as well, making up perhaps one-third of the dinner attenders. The remaining people attending the dinner were mostly congregation members, elders, and staff who came for the purpose of building relationships.

Because of conversations over the meal, the people from the congregation who attended the dinner soon became aware of needs that went beyond food. The homeless people attending the dinner needed warm clothing and blankets as winter approached, so the congregation began collecting those items, as well as toothbrushes and other toiletries to distribute. Some congregation members talked with neighborhood supermarket managers about the needs they were addressing, with the result that the supermarkets donated significant amounts of food. Some of that food went into preparation of the dinners, but some of it was given away at the dinner. The people who regularly attended the dinner formed a loose-knit community.

Indeed, relationships formed between homeless people, food bank patrons, and congregation members, elders, and staff. As a result, the Wednesday dinner community began to spill over to the Sunday morning worshipping community. Because of effective listening at the dinner, congregational leaders became aware that the greatest needs among the poor of their city centered on issues other than food. Housing and jobs were enormous stressors for many of the people in the Wednesday dinner community. And because members of the Wednesday dinner community were increasingly becoming part of the Sunday worshiping community, those same stressors were appearing throughout the congregation.

After the dinner had been going for about seven years, the food bank reached a crisis, precipitated by a number of factors related to the food bank leadership and new policies from the city's network of food banks. The session decided, after a great deal of discussion and prayer, to close the food bank. They also decided to take the money they had been putting into the food bank and add a bit to it, and hire a part-time social worker to help people in both the Wednesday and the Sunday communities with housing and job challenges.

THE MODEL OF LISTENING BY A CONGREGATIONAL SOCIAL WORKER

Jessica was hired for the social worker position and has remained in that position for more than a decade. She spends much of each work day doing a variety of forms of advocacy related to jobs and housing. She might help one person find clothing for a job interview and coach her about what to say in the interview. Next, she might help someone else attempt to find a place to live or help mediate a conflict with a landlord or housemate. One small example of the kind of advocacy she does involved a person who was being evicted because he was accused of bringing bedbugs into his apartment. She helped figure out that the bedbugs were living in the wall, and there was ample evidence they had been there long before the man moved in.

Jessica also does a tremendous amount of listening. She reflected:

> Right now, with the internet and Facebook, it's crucial to listen. No one is really pausing to listen. Even when you go to the doctor these days, they say, "Excuse me" and type notes on the computer. At the same time, we have to acknowledge that it's challenging to be present to people. It's a skill. Most people, instead of listening, start problem solving.

As Jessica has worked with people in need, she has seen over and over that listening validates humanness. "If you can stay present to a person, you are saying to them, 'You are beloved. You matter.' Just be with the person. Stay present. It's so easy for your mind to go off in directions."

She has observed that being cared for through listening is especially significant for people who have been wounded. She has heard so many stories from people who, earlier in their lives, felt invisible or hurt: "They feel their whole personhood wasn't validated when they were younger, and they still feel left out." Out of the people who come to the dinner, she believes that maybe 20 percent simply need to be seen and acknowledged by name. She said she can't remember how many times she's heard someone say something like, "I've been out on the streets since six this morning, and you're the first person to talk to me."

She believes the significance of the dinner doesn't lie in the food provided. She explained:

> We provide a place to meet up with others, a place they can call their own. I love to see signs of ownership of the dinner. Sometimes people come to me with ideas for how we could improve things at the dinner. Instead of listening closely to the detail, which I might disagree with, I realize their concern is a sign of ownership, and I listen carefully to that.

Jessica noted that some of the people she serves have difficulty articulating what they are thinking or feeling.

> Sometimes I'll meet with a person who can't even get out his question. It takes long silences on my part. I try really hard not to think about my laundry list or what I need to get done. I try to stay present and observe what he's doing with his body. I try to reflect back to him what I'm seeing in his body and what I'm hearing. You can miss the point so easily. As a care provider, it's so easy to move along so quickly you miss the point, the main thing on their mind. You can move into problem solving or rescuing, when they need to talk it through and sort it out. You may miss the bigger picture if you move into problem solving too quickly.
>
> When people have been hurt over and over, if you can sit with them and be with them, you communicate that they are beloved of God. You can't tell them God will heal it, or this is happening because they didn't believe. Good kind of listening takes time, and it takes repeated time. Sometimes the time seems ineffective because you're just sitting there with them without talking.

Jessica is an evangelical Christian, committed to proclaiming the Gospel, and she is adamant that proclaiming the Gospel without listening never converts people. She observed that Jesus didn't say, "You need God," at the beginning of conversations. He said it at the end, after listening.

> You have to get really engaged with people before they are willing to listen to you. The Gospel is all about relationships. Relationships only work if you listen one-half to three-quarters of the time. The biggest impact Jesus had was with the Twelve, and he listened to them. Really committed, long-term discipleship involves listening. Short-term conversion is damaging.

Jessica made a remarkable observation. She said that the most "preached to" population in the world is the poor. Many poor people have sat through countless presentations of the Gospel in order to get food, housing, or other help from church-based ministries. "The rich have nothing they need so much that they need to sit through a sermon to get it. People criticize us at our dinners that we don't preach the Gospel enough, but I figure many of the people at our dinners have heard about the Gospel over and over." She believes the truth of the Gospel—our belovedness in God's eyes—is best communicated by careful listening.

A minister who served the congregation and often participated in the dinners believed one of the most significant contributions of the dinner was the provision of a "safe place" where participants could let down and be themselves. Participants felt emotionally safe because they had been welcomed and listened to. That feeling of safety helped them consider taking the risk of thinking about permanent housing or a job. Dinner organizers were also concerned about guests' physical safety. An astonishing percentage of homeless people in the United States have mental health issues. The dinner's leaders encouraged congregational participants at the dinner to pray for physical safety for everyone attending, and leaders were prepared to ask people to leave if they threatened anyone in any way. The commitment of the leaders to physical safety contributed to an atmosphere where participants felt emotionally safe, and the safety of the dinner created space for some participants to reconsider their thoughts and feelings about God. Several individuals came to faith through the dinners and became baptized members of the congregation.

RESPONDING TO NEEDS

How should congregational leaders respond to what they hear in the local community? Some things we hear—such as a story about child or elder abuse, for example—require immediate and concrete action. As Jessica noted, sometimes listening is an end in itself, and we need only to communicate to the speaker that we have truly heard what he or she has said—maybe even nonverbally. But other times, the speaker doesn't feel heard unless we act. For example, if members of a congregation survey their surrounding community and learn that people desperately need good, affordable child care and the congregation does nothing (as far as the neighbors are aware), the neighbors might assume the congregation didn't listen and doesn't care. The lack of response could be worse than if the congregation never listened to its neighbors in the first place.

If a congregation's leaders choose not to act on what they learn from their community, they need to think about how to communicate their decision. Perhaps needs require a level of resources that a congregation might not have. The minister and parish council at St. Stephen's made a strategic choice when they wrote articles for the local newspaper from time to time describing the results of the listening project. The articles laid out the process that the congregation's leaders were engaging in as they responded to what they heard. Perhaps members of the local community were more understanding when the congregation was not able to meet some needs, because the articles described both the thoroughness of the listening process and described the needs the congregation would try, and not try, to meet.

In my interviews, as I asked questions about listening to the local community, I heard several stories about congregations where a small number of people learned about needs in the local community, brought them back to their congregation, and nothing further happened. In one Methodist congregation, for example, the parish council hired two local students to do a listening project. The students were charged with assessing community needs and creating a community profile. At the end of the project, the parish council received the report but ultimately did very little with it. Because the work was done by people who had been hired, very few people in the congregation felt any ownership of the results. In St. Stephen's Parish and Iona Presbyterian Church, on the other hand, the ministers and board members were committed to listening to their local community's needs and responding with discussion, prayer, and action. Commitment to listen and act on the part of a good number of people within the congregation is essential; one or two people who listen to the wider community are seldom enough.

In the preface I mentioned Daniel, a theological college lecturer who teaches evangelism. Daniel advocates a repeating cycle in all forms of mission and ministry: listen—reflect—act—listen—reflect—act. This chapter has presented some examples of what that process looks like for congregations as they interact with the communities around them. The next chapter will build on this topic by discussing issues of discernment, consensus, and listening to God, all of which play a role in processing what's been heard.

QUESTIONS FOR REFLECTION, JOURNALING, AND GROUP DISCUSSION

- Have you seen examples of groups that were given opportunities to listen to the wider community because of unexpected events? If so, what were the results of that listening?
- The first long story in this chapter focused on an intentional listening project by a congregation. The second long story focused on listening while engaging in ministry. What were your reactions to these stories? What aspects of the stories might be helpful as models in your congregation?
- Listening to the wider community requires people who listen, as well as places in the congregation to discuss and pray for what was heard. In what ways are these commitments present in your congregation? What do you think are the strengths and weaknesses of your congregation's listening patterns with respect to the wider community? If you could change one thing about those patterns, what would it be?
- Write a prayer for your congregation as it listens to people beyond its walls. Include in the prayer your desires for yourself as you try to grow in listening to people in the wider community.
- This week, pay someone a compliment for the way he or she listens to people outside your congregation. Ask what priorities or convictions have empowered that kind of listening.

5

LISTENING IN CONSENSUS AND DISCERNMENT

Spiritual discernment, rightly understood, is truly countercultural. It uses silence, it requires that we take our time, it redefines our precious sense of individualism. One other implication of spiritual discernment is a potential redistribution of power. If you must listen to each person with attentiveness because you never know who the Holy Spirit will choose to speak through at any given moment, then we must listen with as much care to a stranger as to a longstanding church member, we must listen as attentively to a young person as to a mature adult. Because you never know.

—Martin B. Copenhaver, "Decide or Discern," in *The Christian Century*[1]

Darren moved to a new city two years ago to be the senior minister of a large urban congregation. The congregation draws from a wide diversity across the socioeconomic spectrum, ranging from homeless people to business executives. Because of the diversity in the congregation, members often cluster with others like them. Several times, Darren has said to the elders something like this:

> Yes, it's cool that we gather here as a church board with diverse people coming from diverse groups. But you're not here merely to bring your own opinion or the opinion of your group. You're here to listen to God with one another on behalf of the whole congregation. The two things are not disconnected, but they are not the same.

Some elders have responded, "I thought I had been elected as elder to represent a constituency of my friends" or "I thought I was elected elder to make changes I thought were necessary." These perspectives are exacerbated by the fact that this board of elders has a history of working out of a corporate model, influenced by the number of business executives who have served as elders over the years. In this congregation, the corporate model means that elders bring their own concerns to meetings and often view their task as describing all possible options, expecting to participate in a kind of bargaining process to decide which option to adopt. Darren has observed, "At the end of meetings, after laying out countless options, we are no closer to knowing where God is guiding us as a group."

The situation at Darren's church illustrates some of the challenges of leadership in congregations today. With decreasing resources, congregations need to be very sure they are engaging in exactly what God is calling them to do instead of committing themselves to scattered activities that don't accomplish their central purpose. Discerning God's call and God's guidance is essential. In many places, however, the congregational culture of decision making has been profoundly influenced by representative democracy and the business culture. Many businesses are moving away from a top-down leadership model, trying to encourage decision making by consensus, which often results in better decisions, because more concerns and issues are addressed. In addition, more perspectives, experience, knowledge, and wisdom are brought to the discussion. In many congregations, the ministers and elders are also moving away—or have already moved away—from top-down leadership or voting, drawing on consensus models brought from the business world and from elsewhere. But is consensus any better than voting or following a strong leader when the goal is to try to discern where God is guiding a congregation? Shifts in leadership practices raise questions, and this chapter will address three of them: What is consensus? How is consensus related to discernment? And what is the role of listening in both?

CONSENSUS

Almost thirty years ago my husband brought home a book that made a significant change in the ways I made decisions with others. The book, *Getting to Yes* by Roger Fisher and William Ury,[2] argues that often we present our ideas and listen to others present their ideas as well, with the expectation that we will choose one of the options that have been presented. Fisher and Ury describe a consensus process in which everyone lays out not only possible plans for action but also the concerns and priorities that lie behind the plans. This allows a pair of individuals or a group to look deeply at those concerns and priorities in order to try to figure out a way that the majority of those issues can be addressed.

Before reading that book, I had viewed decision making with others as a bit of an adversarial process. I usually had my idea, my proposed plan, clearly in mind. The purpose of conversation in decision making was to try to convince my husband, my kids, my brother, my friend, the church committee, or the church board of elders to go along with my plan. I can be quite articulate in laying out reasons why my plan is a good one, and I can (sadly) be quite forceful when I talk about what I have in mind. Fisher and Ury's book urged me to consider another way, to listen to the commitments and passions that lay behind others' plans in order to try to come up with a plan—sometimes something none of us had dreamed of ahead of time—that might address the maximum number of priorities and goals of the people involved.

A small example of the consensus pattern described in *Getting to Yes* comes from my marriage. "Let's go for a bicycle ride," my husband suggests. I respond by saying I'd rather go out to eat. We could (1) discuss the options or argue about which one to do, (2) flip a coin to decide between the two options, or (3) ask what lies behind the suggestion. When we discuss the concerns that lie behind each of our proposals, it turns out my husband wants to get some exercise, and I want to talk over something with him. We decide that going for a walk would meet both of our goals; he can get some exercise and I can talk over my burning issue with him. Neither of us originally proposed a walk, but a walk meets both of our goals.

The English word "consensus" comes from an identical Latin word that means "agreement," and the most common understanding of consensus is general agreement. A decision made by general agreement can involve the style of decision making I used before I read *Getting to Yes*, which emphasized giving rational reasons to convince others that my plan is best. Someone says, "Let's have the treasurer's report at the beginning of the meeting today, so we can know where we stand financially before we discuss the plans for the remodel." The reason given for this change in the agenda is clear and compelling, and everyone at the meeting nods and says, "Fine." A consensus decision has been made. General agreement can also be achieved by voting. In this case, perhaps the moderator asks for a vote, and everyone there, or the overwhelming majority, votes "yes."

Sometimes general agreement is easy to achieve, particularly with straightforward decisions, but often issues in congregations are quite complex. Behind the Latin word *consensus* lies its root word *consentio*, which literally means "feel together." Many group decisions about complex issues, if they're going to reflect general agreement rather than a close vote or the forceful guidance of one person, require some discussion about the feelings, goals, priorities, passions, and concerns that lie behind the proposed action plans. In order for a group of people to "feel together," they must listen carefully to each other.

Consensus decisions can be beneficial for many reasons. Addressing the feelings, goals, priorities, passions, and concerns of a wider number of people usually means that the decision is a better one, that it addresses more issues and needs. Participants feel respected because they have been listened to, which reinforces group cohesiveness and identity. Usually, a large percentage of the people involved feel ownership of the decision, so participants tend to be willing to work hard to see that the decision is implemented. Consensus decisions can build a commitment to the good of the group, rather than the good of an individual or a group the individual represents.

However, consensus decisions can be entirely divorced from the priority Darren posed to his elders: "You're here to listen to God together on behalf of the congregation." Imagine a setting in 2007 where a church board was choosing between two options for a new fellowship hall they were planning to build. One option involved a hall that would easily convert to a gym, and the other option was a more traditional fellowship hall. When talk about a new building started a couple of years earlier, a few people expressed their concerns that perhaps this was not the time to be building anything. They were in the minority at the beginning of the process, and they yielded to the stronger voices and enthusiasm of other board members, so no one felt any urgency to consider their views. The board reached consensus about the fellowship hall/gym option without reconsidering the option of not building anything at this time. They began fundraising and broke ground in late 2007, and then the economic down-turn of 2008 halted the whole process.

If the project had not been started, the congregation would have had more energy and resources to help people in need during the downturn. Hindsight made several elders remember those tentative voices from two years earlier, suggesting that this was not a good time to start a building project. Those elders wondered if inadequate listening may have played a role in making a decision that proved to be problematic. From the begin-ning of the process, were all opinions brought out onto the table, or were the loudest voices most influential? Did anyone talk about discerning God's guidance in the process of making the decision, or did the discus-sion center too much on the wants and desires of the various groups within the church? Was there any openness to a decision other than build-ing one of the two options?

Just because a decision turns out to be problematical in some way doesn't mean God's guidance was absent or that inadequate listening took place. All of our actions take place in a fallen world, so even the wisest decision might not work out perfectly. However, problems raise questions, and these elders were right to discuss those questions and to try to learn from the pattern of past decision making. The elders needed to discuss whether the decision was rushed, less assertive voices were si-lenced, and the emphasis of the discussion centered on meeting the needs of various groups within the church rather than considering the wisdom of the options. Because good consensus depends on some measure of "feeling with" each other, listening well to all participants is essential, and listening well takes a lot of time. Many church boards and commit-tees find it hard to allocate enough time for effective listening.

The elders came to believe that perhaps more prayer and discussion in 2007 about the option of not going ahead might have allowed the board to hear God's guidance to wait. At the time, because the process was con-ducted by consensus, the board members felt they must be responding to God's will. However, consensus and discernment of God's guidance are not the same thing. Consensus plays a significant role in the discernment process, but consensus can enable a group to decide among several op-tions that are all undesirable and do not reflect God's priorities. Consen-sus helps a group reach decisions that most or all members of a group agree with, that meet the needs or convictions of most of the group members. How is discernment different?

DISCERNMENT

Some of the synonyms associated with discernment reveal the essential components of discernment that may not be present in consensus decisions: acumen, keen judgment, wisdom, and insight. Consensus focuses on meeting the largest possible number of needs, while discernment is centered on figuring out the wisest decision. In Christian congregations, where leaders and members believe that wisdom comes from God, discernment is usually connected with hearing and responding to God's guidance. Tim Challies, a Canadian pastor and popular blogger, has proposed a definition of discernment that works well for congregational leadership groups:

> Discernment is a process of prayerful reflection which leads a person or community to understanding of God's call at a given time or in particular circumstances of life. It involves listening to God in all the ways God communicates with us: in prayer, in the scriptures, through the Church and the world, in personal experience, and in other people. [3]

Discernment is rooted in listening to God, and the various ways God speaks to us are laid out clearly in this definition.

Discernment, in fact, requires a strong investment in listening to God as individuals and together, which involves spending significant amounts of time in prayer, studying the Bible, including pondering the life and ministry of Jesus, and paying attention to ways God has worked and is working in the congregation. Our own desires, priorities, opinions, and passions play a role, but they are not the only factors considered. In addition, discernment takes into consideration the patterns of congregational life and God's past guidance into those patterns, as well as the inner nudges that people are receiving from God. In the next chapter, I'll present ways to hear God's voice communally through the Bible, and in chapter 7, I'll discuss numerous spiritual practices that allow groups to pray together for guidance from God. Discernment doesn't happen just because people want it to or talk about its importance; it requires a significant commitment of time and attention.

The definition above emphasizes that discernment involves understanding God's call in a specific circumstance. Another way to look at discernment emphasizes choosing between right and wrong, or good and evil. One of the blog posts I read about this second form of discernment referred twice to differentiating between good and evil in order to live an "uncompromising life." That blogger emphasized discernment as "the ability to think biblically about all areas of life."[4] For congregational leaders who are striving to make a wise decision, guided by God, in a specific challenge facing their congregation, however, the language of differentiating between right and wrong or good and evil does not work well. Listening carefully to others' feelings, priorities, and concerns involves suspending those kinds of judgments. Each person on any church board or committee has the potential to hear God's voice for the group. In order to cultivate an appreciation for that still, small voice among people who might not feel very comfortable expressing what they think they may have heard from God, group members need to adopt a posture of gentleness and openness, not an attitude that readily leaps to judgments of good and evil. However, I like the blogger's emphasis on the ability to think biblically about all areas of life. So often committee and board decisions in congregations are divorced from prayer and scripture.

One of my interviewees, a spiritual director who teaches practical theology at an Anglican theological college, reinforced the idea that listening to God as a group involves suspending judgment. She advocated that a discernment process needs to begin with an affirmation that we want to know God's will here, that we are examining God's call to us. Some of the components of a discernment process that she mentioned include: inviting people to dream dreams, taking in all information relevant to the issue, making a real commitment to prayer, inviting everyone involved into prayerful openness, prayerfully considering what is going on in the congregation, and viewing each suggestion on its own merits rather than against other suggestions.

She recommended that each participant in a discernment process pay attention to their thoughts related to "oughts" and "shoulds," which are not good indicators of God's voice when they feel heavy and burdensome. Instead, she suggested that each person look within to try to identify the sources of energy that say, "I'd love to do that." That kind of energy, she argued, helps groups identify the path where God is leading. She stressed that listening skills are required to pick up the presence of that energy. She advocated that each person be given a turn to speak, saying, "This is what I feel or sense." A discernment process is not a debate pro or con, but a chance to weigh and reflect. She noted, "When people are really trying to listen to each other and to God, they take note of each person's words and each person's feelings."

Jane, a minister and theological college lecturer, noted that listening to God is both the easiest and hardest thing we do. To do the will of God we have to discern it, and at one level we know this, but doing it isn't as easy as talking about it.

Discernment isn't a quick process, and we so often want to do it in a half hour.

One of my interviewees, a children's ministries director in a large church, remembers a senior minister she worked with for many years. She observed a pattern in the way he led church board meetings. He almost never brought forward an agenda item that needed to be decided at that meeting. As often as possible, he introduced items one, two, or even three months before the decision would have to be made, and he encouraged elders to pray for God's guidance during the intervening months. This approach cultivated an attitude that God's guidance was the key issue, that discerning God's guidance took time, and that spending time in discernment was worth every moment it took.

An associate minister in a mid-sized church remembers when a new senior minister arrived a few years ago.

> The congregation expected he would cast a vision and help us figure out where to go. To the surprise of the lay leaders, he told them, "God knows where he is calling us to go, and we'll try to hear his voice together." Some of the lay leaders were quite frustrated, because they assumed he would lead them somewhere, not lead them into a discernment process.

Did their frustration come because it's easier to be told what to do? Did they resist the kind of effort required to discern together? Communal discernment requires a great deal of effort. Frankly, voting or following a strong leader requires less effort on everyone's part. Communal discernment requires an intentional commitment on the part of leaders, and numerous factors and practices in a congregation contribute to a congregational culture that encourages discernment. Nurturing this kind of congregational culture takes time and effort.

CONGREGATIONAL CULTURE AND DISCERNMENT

Several of my interviewees talked about the many components in congregations that affirm the value of discernment. Kate, an Anglican curate, cited her home church, which emphasizes discernment. Permeating the ethos of that congregation is a commitment to listening to God. Kate reported that her congregation engages in numerous practices in order to cultivate a culture of listening to God. She used the word "multi-factorial" to describe the ways her home congregation nurtures this listening posture. Some of those factors—or practices—are:

- an intentional commitment to listening to God, stated in numerous settings
- sermons that model and discuss listening to God
- prayer, including periods of listening, at meetings
- collaborative leadership and openness to hearing God's voice through different people
- leadership groups stopping to talk about vision and mission, making sure specific strategies are rooted there
- parish council retreat days
- encouragement for lay leaders to listen to God and to each other
- encouragement for all members to seek God's guidance about where God is calling them to serve

"In that congregation," she said, "listening to God is in the fabric of how it is. You have to make intentional choices, but it's simply assumed that that everyone will try to listen for God's voice." She contrasted her home congregation with a congregation where she served as curate. That congregation, she said, was characterized by fears that resources were always going to be scarce for them, which impacted their ability to listen for God's guidance. They feared receiving any new visions from God or from members of the congregation, because they were sure they wouldn't have enough resources to act on those visions. Because of her experience in her home congregation, however, she is convinced that "if we listen to God and God's vision, God will provide the resources and we don't have to be afraid."

Another limiting factor Kate observed in the congregation where she served related to the senior minister's lack of interest in hearing God's voice. Based on her experience in her home congregation, she believes

> there has to be an emphasis and openness to hearing God for everyone. But will be influenced by the leader. Someone has to lead, and the leader has to be open to hearing from God. This is key. You can't be a visionary group if your leader isn't open to that.

Melanie, a spiritual director, is another person who has experienced a congregation where leaders and members expect to experience God's guidance and where discernment of God's leading is a strong component of the congregation's culture. She has observed that listening to God requires time for reflection, and in a busy culture we often don't have time. She expressed concern that because we're bombarded with an ever-increasing number of stimuli, listening will become more difficult. She stressed that listening to God involves observing connections—between events in our own lives, others' lives, and scripture—and the "Aha!" moment when we see those connections requires a "prayerful, contemplative stance toward life. It's a reflective posture. You have to be settled to listen and to watch for answers to the prayer, 'God, give us eyes to see where you've been present.'"

Her congregation has been shaped by several ministers who stressed listening to God. Melanie remembers one of them who frequently mentioned in sermons the need to pay attention to God's voice and God's guidance. She said:

> That might have been his one main sermon. He stressed that listening is intentional. You can't just assume you're a good listener. He stressed that listening is connected to your own prayer: "Show me, help me see what you're doing." Listening requires a posture of humility, an emphasis that it's not about me, it's about taking in what God is doing. You can't be obsessed with what you'll say next. Listening requires an incarnational posture, where you believe God can speak to you through someone else, and God can show love to you through someone else. Listening to God, in fact, requires taking a risk.

Indeed, risk is inherent in assuming a humble posture, because if life isn't centered on me, the someone who is at the center might have some surprising and challenging priorities. When we pray "Help me see what you're doing," we are inviting a new perspective, sometimes in a small way and sometimes in a huge and life-changing paradigm shift. An incarnational posture, believing that God is present in the people around me and might speak to me through them, also involves risk, because I might hear something unexpected that will demand a new and uncomfortable response.

These two congregations that encourage a culture of discerning God's guidance have numerous characteristics that contribute to their ethos. Listening to God is emphasized in sermons, practiced at meetings, modeled by the senior minister and congregational leaders, and encouraged for all members. Indeed, nurturing such an ethos is multifactorial and involves listening in many different settings. The characteristics of these congregations also raise an important question: How can we be sure that a group of people is actually hearing God and not the voices of group members' own desires and opinions?

THE ROLE OF CONSENSUS IN DISCERNMENT

Under the Banner of Heaven, a book by Jon Krakauer, is the most powerfully disturbing account I have ever read that illustrates the possible confusion between our own desires and God's guidance. Krakauer tells the true-crime story of two brothers who felt led by God to kill their sister-in-law and her fifteen-month-old daughter.[5] The brutal incident happened in 1984, and the two brothers were part of a fundamentalist group that had broken off from the Mormon Church.

As I read the book, a part of me wanted to argue that for many reasons, nothing like that could happen among the people of faith I know. Another part of me was deeply disturbed by the fact that the language the two brothers used to describe hearing God's voice and being convinced about God's guidance was very similar to the language I have heard in many churches. The book raised big questions: If we are going to insist that discerning God's leading and hearing God's voice is a significant and necessary part of congregational leadership today, what are the safeguards? What are the boundaries that keep us from following paths that we think come from God but in reality do not?

These questions bring us back to the issue of consensus, an essential part of any congregational discernment process. As I wrote earlier, consensus by itself is no guarantee that God's call is being sought; consensus can be a process that focuses on meeting the greatest number of felt needs in a group, and felt needs sometimes have no connection with God's priorities. However, when a group desires to seek God's guidance, they must understand principles of consensus building in order to discuss the various ways people in the group are hearing God's voice. Human beings often hear God's voice partially, faintly, or indistinctly—rather than clearly—similar to the way we see God, as the apostle Paul wrote in 1 Corinthians 13:12: "For now we see in a mirror, dimly." Members of a group seeking to hear and follow God can bring their partial, faint, and indistinct sense of what God is saying, and the group, by consensus, can try to get a fuller picture of God's guidance.

Reaching consensus as a part of a discernment process requires many of the same components as any kind of consensus process, with a major difference being that the process is focused on reaching general agree-ment about where and how God is guiding the group rather than on how the greatest number of needs can be met. The leader of the group needs to encourage all members to contribute, because God can speak to anyone, young or old, experienced or inexperienced. The leader needs to encour-age everyone to talk about not only possible plans and projects, but the priorities, passions, and goals that they sense might contribute to under-standing God's guidance in this situation. Those priorities, passions, and goals might come from pondering God's acts and Jesus' ministry in the Bible, conversations with congregation members, an understanding of Christian history or the wider church, our own experiences, or inner nudges.

Achieving consensus in a discernment process might involve stopping for a time of prayer, spoken or silent, or stopping for someone to read a passage from the Bible that has come to their mind and that might reflect God's priorities. Reaching consensus in a discernment process might re-quire adjourning for a coffee break, or for a week or a month, to allow everyone the opportunity for reflection and prayer.

Reaching consensus about what God is saying to a group is no guaran-tee that God's voice has been heard clearly, but it is the best we can do. After I read *Under the Banner of Heaven*, I was troubled for months as I pondered the terrifying reality that anyone can do anything with the con-viction of having heard God's direction. Making decisions as a group helps to guard against misunderstanding God's direction. No congregational leader wants to participate in a murder because someone feels God leading him that way, and I trust no congregational leader would do that. But we are tempted to rush into unwise plans and programs, and we are prone to act too quickly because something sounds plausible. I ultimately came to the conclusion that even though terrible things can be done in the name of God, congregations still need to embrace the goal of following God's general guidance from the Bible and God's specific guidance for each congregation, which come through nudges, passions, words, and pictures given by God to leaders and members. We are called to do the best we can to follow God, individually and communally.

AN EXAMPLE OF COMMUNAL DISCERNMENT

I serve on the national workgroup that assesses candidates for ordained ministry for the Presbyterian Church in New Zealand. When I was asked to participate just over two years ago, I agreed with enthusiasm, because I was eager to experience an intense group discernment process. I've now attended the yearly assessment weekend twice.

We typically have about a dozen candidates, and they gather with the fifteen members of the assessment workgroup for a weekend at a retreat center. The candidates can bring their spouse or another support person. During the weekend, the candidates give two speeches and participate in two group projects. Two assessment workgroup members interview each candidate about sense of call, and another two members interview each candidate about life experience. Each assessor assigns a numerical score for each candidate's speech, participation in the group projects, and interview. After the candidates leave at the end of the weekend, the assessors hear psychologists' reports and recommendations from presbytery representatives. Then the "discernment process" begins.

We spend thirty to seventy-five minutes discussing each candidate. The numerical scores are taken into consideration, and the assessors who interviewed the candidates talk about the interviews. Any of the assessors can mention things they observed in the speeches, group exercises, or casual conversations at mealtimes. The moderator makes sure that each of the fifteen assessors has the opportunity to speak up. As the conversation about each candidate begins to wind down, we spend several minutes in silence for personal reflection and prayer. Then we vote. In order to advance toward ordination studies, each candidate must receive an 80 percent positive vote.

Over the years, the assessors have chosen the 80 percent figure as a good indicator of group consensus. One hundred percent agreement is simply too hard to achieve in the time allotted. But a simple majority vote doesn't seem to represent consensus about God's call to an individual. This example illustrates that voting can be used as a part of a discernment process, but the vote must be significantly higher than 50 percent in order to indicate consensus about God's guidance.

In my two years of participating in this process, I have experienced a change of mind about a candidate several times as I have listened to what the other assessors have perceived about the candidate. I trust that they are discerning things about the candidate, and about God's work in the candidate's life, that I simply have not perceived. My votes are informed by my own observations and perceptions, what I hear from others, and inner nudges that seem to come from God.

An assessment weekend on behalf of a whole denomination is not identical to a decision-making process in a congregation, but some of the principles carry over to congregational settings. Each person is committed to trying to discern God's call. Gathering information—in this case from psychologists, presbytery leaders, academic transcripts, medical reports, and other places—always plays a role in discerning God's guidance, as does listening carefully to the perceptions and observations of the other people involved in discerning. Before the weekend, each of us in the assessment workgroup reads summaries of the candidates' profiles, and we pray individually about the candidates and the whole process. Our meetings before the weekend involve a few times of spoken prayer together, asking for God's guidance. During the discernment process we pray silently for several minutes about each candidate. We try to listen inwardly for God's voice.

I'm sure the candidates are quite happy that we spend a lot of time assessing them, rather than doing it quickly, but for the assessors the process is long and tiring. I have found that the assessment and discernment process is also deeply satisfying because of the care taken to try to discern what God is doing throughout the process. That satisfaction flows over to other areas of my life and renews my commitment to be a person who seeks to listen to God.

Throughout this chapter, the role of listening in discernment and consensus has been articulated and illustrated in numerous ways. The phrase "double listening" has been used in several ways in this book, and the role of listening in consensus related to discernment definitely involves a form of double listening: each individual needs to listen to God in their own hearts and mind, and they need to listen to each other's perceptions of the voice of God. The next two chapters will present more options for groups who want to discern God's voice in congregational decisions.

Congregational discernment involves a desire to hear and respond to God's vision, even though it may be quite challenging to discern exactly what that vision is. The goal is definitely worthy of pursuit. These themes are visible in comments from two of my interviewees. One minister noted a frequent temptation for church leadership groups: "There's a big difference between asking God to bless our vision and listening for his vision and working that out." Jane, a theological college lecturer, views "a really good church meeting" as a place where "we encourage Christian people to offer their contribution, while expecting the community to test whether something is of God, without 'knocking the stuffing' out of the people who have contributed."

QUESTIONS FOR REFLECTION, JOURNALING, AND GROUP DISCUSSION

- In your congregation or in other groups you've participated in, what have you observed about the pros and cons of the three ways of making decisions mentioned in this chapter: voting, reaching consensus, and trying to discern God's guidance?
- Where and in what settings have you experienced God speaking to you or nudging you as an individual? Does God speak to you most often through words, such as the Bible, sermons, or words of friends? Does God speak to you most often through nature, your body, or other non-verbal means? Spend some time pondering these patterns in your life.
- In what ways does your congregation encourage people to listen to God? In what ways do communal listening to God and communal discernment play a role in leadership decisions? In what ways would you like to nurture a greater commitment to communal discernment?

- Write a prayer for your congregation related to its decision-making patterns. What do you long for? Hope for? Express those hopes and longings in a prayer. In the prayer, include your desires for yourself as you participate in making decisions with others.
- Think about people in your life who have modeled an ability to listen to God. This week, pay a compliment to one of those people and ask that person what factors helped teach that receptive, humble posture of listening.

6

LISTENING TO GOD TOGETHER THROUGH SCRIPTURE

And now, my children, listen to me: happy are those who keep my ways. Hear instruction and be wise, and do not neglect it. Happy is the one who listens to me, watching daily at my gates, waiting beside my doors.
—Proverbs 8:32–34

Then [Jesus] called the crowd again and said to them, "Listen to me, all of you, and understand."
—Mark 7:14

I am twenty years old, a junior in college, and newly recommitted to the Christian faith. I'm spending my spring break at a retreat. I've been to one weekend retreat, but this one lasts five days, and I'm a bit overwhelmed that I have chosen to give my entire spring break to Bible study. The leader of the retreat tells us he trained as an architect and still occasionally designs a building, even though his primary job now is student ministry. He says he's going to teach us a kind of Bible study called "manuscript study."[1]

We're going to study Galatians this week, and the words from the Bible have been typed with wide margins, double spaced. Chapter and verse numbers have been omitted. Each of us has been given a copy, and I have to admit, the whole thing does look like a manuscript. We were encouraged to bring colored pencils and felt-tip pens to the retreat, and the leader suggests we use them to mark up the manuscript. We might want to circle repeated words with different colors or underline sentences we think are important, he says. We might want to write comments in the margins. His training in architecture made him a visual person, and he tells us he has enjoyed marking up many "manuscripts" of Bible passages.

After a prayer asking for God's presence and illumination, the leader gives us forty-five minutes to study the first page on our own. "Just observe," he says. "Pay attention to anything you notice that you think is important or that jumps out at you." At first the minutes drag, and I'm a bit tentative about writing on the clean pages, but then I pull out a red pencil to mark everything the apostle Paul says about himself, and I use blue pencil to underline everything he says about the Galatians. I discover that the word "gospel" is repeated numerous times, and I circle it in orange. The orange circles enable me to notice the repeated pattern in the way the word is used. Hey, this is fun!

The leader puts us in small groups for another forty-five minutes and asks us to talk about what we have observed. When we get back into a large group, he leads a discussion about what we noticed. He draws us out. He makes connections between the things that various students say, and at one point he asks us to talk about the questions the passage raises for us. We break for lunch, and in the afternoon, we repeat the pattern with the next section of Galatians: time alone, time in a small group, then a large group discussion. The whole week goes by in a three-beat rhythm, and we move through the entire letter.

I've never experienced anything like this. In the church of my childhood, someone was always telling me about the Bible or about God. No one encouraged me to ask questions or express my own thoughts or feelings. No one drew me out or considered my observations about the Bible to be worthy of comment. In the year since I have made a recommitment to Christ, I've listened to quite a few people speak about what the Bible says, and I've participated in a small group Bible study. However, I've never been encouraged to study the Bible on my own with colored pencils in hand, and I've never been in a large group setting where I was invited to ask questions and make connections between ideas. I love the process, and I find myself marking up my manuscript with abandon. I jump in enthusiastically during the discussion in both the small and large groups.

I've always been a conscientious, rule-based person who tries to do a good job at everything. Galatians brings me face to face with my desire to prove myself worthy, to justify myself to God and to others by what I do. Galatians introduces me to grace, and my life is transformed. I come back from spring break with a lightness in my step and a deep joy in my heart. I am loved by God, and I don't have to work so hard to try to earn approval. I have learned how to speak a new language, the language of God's acceptance and grace, and it permeates the way I talk and the way I live. In addition, I find I'm bringing new skills to the weekly Bible study I'm attending. I find I look more deeply at the passage, and I'm more able to make connections with my own life.

HEARING GOD'S VOICE IN SCRIPTURE

I hope everyone reading this book has had a moment like mine when the Bible comes alive and God speaks into the issues of everyday life. I hope every reader has experienced the joy of studying the Bible in a group and receiving insights through the observations others make and the energy of group discussion. Numerous factors contributed to my ability to hear God speak to me through the Galatians, in the company of others:

- prayer: every session began with a prayer expressing our dependence on the Holy Spirit to make the words of Galatians clear and life-transforming
- expectation: everyone there expected to learn something from God through studying Galatians
- time alone and together: we had time alone for pondering and time together for discussion
- using our hands and eyes: using colored pencils and felt-tip pens to write all over the pages gave us fresh eyes, and fresh eyes are essential in order to hear God's voice through the Bible
- validation: every person's contribution was valued
- a good leader: the leader was gifted at building on participants' comments and weaving them together

One additional factor relates to the time after the retreat. When I came back to my own campus, the handful of students who had attended the retreat with me were there to talk to. None of them had experienced Galatians as intensely as I did, but all of them had grown spiritually because of the retreat, and I enjoyed debriefing with them.

The ability to hear God communally through Scripture is a key component of the kind of listening needed in congregations in our time. This has always been true. In these rapidly changing and confusing times, we need to hear God's direction for our congregations as much as ever, and the Bible is a primary way that God speaks into our world. I will give several examples of the ways congregations are listening communally to God through the words of the Bible.

"PARTNERS IN PREACHING"

Helen, a Presbyterian minister, has developed a pattern for Bible study with congregation members that aids her sermon preparation, helps participants spend some time with the sermon scripture, and enables everyone to listen for God's voice in a communal setting. In the middle of each week, she gathers for an hour with anyone in the congregation who wishes to participate. No homework is required, and she brings handouts to the gathering with the sermon scripture printed in two columns, on the left side the New Revised Standard Version and in the right hand column *The Message* translation. She asks participants to leave their Bibles at home so they don't look at the notes.

She sets two ground rules for discussion. No one can dominate, and everyone needs to work hard at listening to the text and to others. She asks participants to look for things in the passage that jump out at them, using questions such as: "What bugs you? What shimmers? What confounds you?" When people get off track, she says, "I think we're going down a rabbit trail. Let's go back to the text." She might re-ask a question specific to the passage or say, "What else is hitting you here? What else is tapping you on the shoulder? Causing befuddlement?"

Helen has engaged in this practice at three churches she has served. She reflected:

> One of my passions is to listen to the text together. It takes a while for people to learn to do that. In the beginning, they say, "Preacher, tell me what it means." It's so impactful when people start to listen together. Something inspired starts happening. One week we're listening to the

text, the next week people come back and say, "You won't believe what happened to me and how it relates to our discussion last week."

Those words spoken to Helen illustrate that Bible studies are one more place where people in congregations talk about the intersection of their faith and daily life. In this instance, that overlap comes from listening carefully to the Bible and bringing insights and observations into daily life.

Helen particularly appreciates the way this kind of discussion breaks down barriers and puts everyone in an equal position. "No one person has the single truth. This kind of study builds respect and community. The person you had pegged turns out not to be in that box." Helen is particularly concerned about the polarization of discussion in the public sphere. She mentioned a book on that topic, *The Big Sort: Why the Clustering of Like-Minded America Is Tearing Us Apart* by Bill Bishop,[2] and she believes the subtitle is a good way to describe what's happening in American culture. She has found that discussing the Bible together builds bridges between people who thought they were hopelessly divided by differing opinions. Some of that comes from the attitude Helen takes as she leads the studies. When people say something that might be divisive, she responds with, "Tell us about that," and sometimes, "Let's just try to love one another, and that will take us places we didn't know we wanted to go."

Helen would like to see every small group and committee engaging with the Bible communally. "This kind of study is not telling participants what to think. It's the Spirit working, and Scripture is transformative." Helen finds her weekly study helps her as much as the participants. She said something that is worth pondering in our individualistic culture: "I'm social in the way I hear God speak. I don't do it well alone." I believe many of the people in our congregations are like Helen, longing for a way to hear God with others. Bible study in small groups can help meet that longing. And I believe leadership groups and committees in congregations need to spend some time considering how they could read or study the Bible together, seeking to hear God's voice communally as leaders.

The skill and priorities of the leader definitely make a difference in group discussions of the Bible. Judy, a Presbyterian minister, described a church where she had done an internship. The minister led a Bible study each week on the lectionary passages he would preach on the following

Sunday. Judy was excited to get to know the people in the congregation by discussing the lectionary passages with them, but she rapidly found that the Bible study consisted almost entirely of the minister talking about the passage and the participants listening. Another interviewee told me about the Bible study groups in her church, many of them led by the minister, who goes into each study with a very specific point he wanted the participants to get from the Bible. A strong agenda on the part of the leader shuts down discussion, and does not permit insights from the passage to bubble up from the participants.

LECTIO DIVINA

The theme of letting the meaning of the passage come from the participant's pondering is very relevant to the contemplative practice of *lectio divina*, as is the wonderful reality that people of opposing political and theological views find themselves enjoying each other as they meditate on a passage of scripture and then share their thoughts. I have heard wonderful stories about groups of people encountering God, as well as each other, through communal experiences of *lectio divina*.

The Latin words simply mean "sacred reading," and the notion of reading the Bible slowly and meditatively dates back at least 1,500 years. The four movements we use today in *lectio divina* were formalized in the twelfth century. When I learned *lectio divina*, the leader prepared a handout with a scripture passage of about three to ten verses on the top of the page, and the four movements of *lectio divina* at the bottom, like this:

- *Lectio* (read). Read the passage slowly, watching for a word or phrase that jumps out or shines.
- *Meditatio* (meditate). Ponder the meaning of the word or phrase that struck you.
- *Oratio* (pray). Pray from the heart in response to the text, any kind of prayer: adoration, thanksgiving, intercession, confession, lament, etc.
- *Contemplatio* (contemplate). Wait for God to speak to you, perhaps in an image or metaphor.

The leader invited one or two people to read the passage aloud, and then we spent ten to fifteen minutes in silence, working through the movements on our own. After the period of silence, the leader would invite anyone who wanted to talk about the experience to do so, with no pressure to speak. I always found it amazing to hear the diversity of things people noticed in the passage, often quite different from what I had focused on.

In my interviews for my book *Joy Together*, I heard from several lay leaders and ministers who have adapted *lectio divina* to allow for more group discussion.[3] Some of them use the same four movements but allow time for brief conversation about each movement after a period of silent reflection. Some of them use silence for two or three of the movements, with discussion after each period of silence, but for one or two of the movements they dispense with silence and move right into discussion. One leader often combines two of the movements, making the whole process involve three movements rather than four. Some of these leaders use directed questions for each of the four movements, rather than the more general instructions I have listed above. In all cases, these leaders ask at least two people to read the passage aloud before any silence or discussion, and hearing the passage read aloud more than once has significant impact.

Lectio divina helps us focus carefully and prayerfully on a portion of the Bible. It provides a structure for slowing down and paying attention to what God might be saying through these words. Professor of spiritual theology Gabriel O'Donnell describes it as "a disciplined form of devotion and not a method of Bible study. It is done purely and simply to come and to know God, to be brought before His Word, to listen."[4] When done in a group setting, this listening benefits us as individuals because the companionship of others in the group encourages us to listen more deeply, and their insights contribute to our own perception of what God is saying. The conversation among participants also benefits the group, because bridges are built between people who might not normally have much in common.

OTHER COMMUNAL SETTINGS

Many kinds of small group and large group settings—ranging from structured to informal—can provide opportunities for listening to God communally through the Bible. I believe it is important not to set up a false dichotomy between academic study of the Bible and a willingness to hear from God, who can and does speak through many different forms of focusing on scripture, including academic study. However, most of us need encouragement to listen for God's priorities, call, and voice of love as we approach the Bible. It's simply too easy to remain in analytical mode when discussing the Bible. In addition to small group Bible studies, group discussion related to lectionary passages, and *lectio divina*, my interviewees talked about several other communal settings where people hear from God through the Bible and are encouraged to interact with each other about what they are hearing.

Sermons

Preachers will be happy to hear that many of my interviewees talked about hearing God speak to them through sermons. A wide variety of books address the many ways preachers can help worshippers hear the Bible speak through sermons, and perhaps an entire chapter of this book should have been devoted to that topic. Instead, I have chosen to focus here on the ways congregations provide opportunities for worshippers to interact with others about the sermon. Some, perhaps most, of that interaction happens informally. "What did you think of the sermon?" is a common question at coffee hour and even in mid-week encounters when the sermon was controversial or memorable in some way. In the chapter on listening in congregations, I mentioned a small group that enjoys going out for coffee together after church, and they frequently discuss the sermon over coffee and a pastry. The challenge, always, in discussions about the sermon is to move from a cognitive analysis of the ideas in the sermon to a focus on hearing God's voice through the scripture preached.

Some congregations provide structures to encourage worshippers to reflect on the sermon. Some congregations set aside a time and place after the worship service for sermon discussion. Several congregations in my city meet café-style around tables. Typically, the worship leader asks participants to chat around the table at some point early in the service about a question related to everyday life. A second time of casual conversation around the tables often happens after the sermon, with the opportunity to respond to something in the sermon. A friend told me about her father, a minister in the Midwest, who prepares detailed discussion questions for small groups every Sunday as a part of his sermon preparation process. The small groups in his congregation discuss the same passage from the Bible each week following the sermon on that passage, using the questions prepared by the minister.

I visited a church with an open microphone after the sermon. The Sunday I was there, about ten people got up to say something brief. Several reported answers to prayer, several requested prayer for something, and one person thanked the congregation for helping with an event at the church the previous week. A couple of people said something they appreciated from the sermon. A friend of mine who attends that church estimated that about eight to twelve people usually speak up during that time. She told me that the response to the sermon might include disagreement or discussion of particular points. The worship leader prays after everyone has spoken. My friend noted,

> The folk who lead are usually very good at bringing everything together before God—discussion, observations, prayer requests, and things to be thankful for. It's also usually one of the last things that happens in the service, so pretty soon thereafter we stand and sing a blessing to each other.

I really like the idea of a communal prayer that enfolds the comments about the sermon.

Retreats

Retreats provide a variety of wonderful opportunities for communal engagement with a part of the Bible. I have experienced retreats where participants studied a short book of the Bible or two to three chapters of a longer book, with lots of discussion and interaction in small groups and the large group. I have also experienced quiet, meditative retreats centered on *lectio divina* and other forms of contemplative prayer, perhaps focused on a few psalms or other prayers in the Bible or perhaps involving praying the Psalms. Many retreats with a central focus on a topic or an issue include times of personal devotion, particularly in the morning, centered on a passage from the Bible. In some cases the retreat speaker later reflects on that passage, or participants discuss the passage in small groups.

My spiritual director recently told me about a retreat she took with two other women. Her experience presented a whole new paradigm for listening to God through scripture in a retreat setting. For four days, the women spent three hours in the morning and three hours in the afternoon each day interacting with one verse from the Gospel of John. In each three-hour block, they spent ninety minutes alone meditating and journaling about the verse. Then they gathered to share their reflections for ninety minutes. My spiritual director felt that six hours of quiet pondering and discussing each verse was not enough, because she experienced a seemingly endless depth of meaning and application in each verse. That is a common fruit of a contemplative approach to the Bible, but I had never heard about such an intense focus on so few verses, and I would love to try it one day.

Learning the Sweep of Biblical History

Recently a friend told me about his most meaningful encounter with the Bible in a group. He attended a Bible college, and in his first year he was required to take a yearlong course that presented an overview of biblical history from beginning to end. He said the teacher was so good, and the story so interesting, that many times he felt emotionally connected to the people and events. For example, the pain of the exile in the sixth century B.C. became so real to him that when the Israelites under Nehemiah rejoiced over rebuilding Jerusalem's wall, he found himself rejoicing as well. His eyes filled with tears, and he had the sense of becoming a participant in the story through his imagination.

My friend believes that part of why people have difficulty experiencing God's presence and hearing God's voice through the Bible is that they don't understand the sweep and flow of the biblical story. Without that understanding, any given passage from the Bible lacks a sense of setting, and the bigger purpose is obscured. Some Christians are trying to address this lack by putting together dramas or lectures that provide that kind of overview of biblical history. Bible studies on passages like Nehemiah 9, Psalm 136, or Acts 7 can provide a helpful starting place.

HEARING GOD SPEAK

Several of my interviewees mentioned that we often think we know what the Bible says. In order to hear God's voice, they stressed that we have to read it as if for the first time. I am struck by the parallel here with listening in any conversation. When we think we know what our conversation partner will say, our listening is impeded. Recently in my own congregation, before a sermon on listening to God, the minister asked us to gather in groups of three or four to talk about obstacles to hearing God speak. The others in my small group brought up several obstacles. "We're afraid God will demand something of us that we don't want to do," one person said, and another person amplified that statement: "We're afraid God's going to send us to Africa!" Another person said, "Sometimes I don't feel worthy or capable of hearing God." Any leader who wants to create a congregational culture characterized by a sense of anticipation about hearing God's voice through the Bible needs to address common obstacles.

One additional comment from that Sunday morning service focused on listening to God stimulated my thinking. "We don't expect to hear God speak," one person said. According to several of my interviewees, we live in a time of low biblical literacy, which contributes to a lack of expectancy that God's voice might be heard through a book viewed by many as outdated, misogynistic, paternalistic, and irrelevant. Even within communities of faith, some members have no expectation that the Bible will be much more than tangentially relevant to everyday life. This increases the significance of conversations that show the overlap of faith and everyday life, particularly when those conversations are based in or informed by God's voice through the Bible. Creating settings for such conversations needs to be a priority for congregational leaders.

Congregations do create many settings for listening to God together through scripture, including sermons and sermon reflection times, small group Bible studies, retreats, and opportunities to reflect quietly on scripture and then share thoughts. These participatory experiences make room for insights from young and old, men and women, and people with differing levels of income and education. Careful listening in these settings builds bridges between people with different political and theological convictions, because God's voice is the great leveler, inviting us to share in the journey of life together as fellow pilgrims.

QUESTIONS FOR REFLECTION, JOURNALING, AND GROUP DISCUSSION

- In what ways has God spoken to you most clearly through the Bible, for example, through sermons, small groups, personal study, or in some other setting? In what ways have conversations with others contributed to your ability to hear God's voice in the Bible? For you personally, what are the obstacles to hearing God speak through the Bible?
- When you think of people in your congregation listening to God through scripture, what settings come to mind? In what ways might you encourage your congregation to make more opportunities to listen to God's voice in the Bible together?
- When you think of your congregation, what do you perceive as the greatest obstacles to expecting to hear God speak through the Bible? Can you think of some ways to address those obstacles?
- Write a prayer for yourself as a listener to God's voice in scripture. What do you long for? Express that longing in your prayer.
- This week pay a compliment to someone who has modeled listening to God in Scripture to you.

7

LISTENING TO GOD TOGETHER THROUGH SPIRITUAL PRACTICES

True prayer is a life of radical availability to God in the world.
—M. Robert Mulholland Jr., "Prayer as Availability to God," *Weavings*[1]

In 2005 I wrote a book on fasting. I had fasted in numerous ways on my own, and I had read widely on the subject, but I knew I needed stories for my book. So I sent an email to just about everyone I know, asking them questions about their experiences with fasting and requesting contact information for their friends who fast. The emails poured in, dozens of them, containing many stories and themes that surprised me. Many of my friends and acquaintances fast, but they never talk about it, trying to keep quiet about fasting as Jesus commanded in Matthew 6:16–18. Many of them fast with others. Many of them fast from things other than food, such as music, shopping, lattes, entertainment or news media, eating in restaurants, even makeup.

Many of them described intense and clear experiences of hearing God's voice and guidance when they fast. A lot of the stories about hearing God's voice so clearly came from individuals—friends and acquaintances of mine in the United States—who had fasted alone. However, several people described fasting with groups for the purpose of receiving guidance from God for their congregations or ministry communities. Those stories mostly came from Africa, South and Central America, and

Asia, contacts given to me by friends and acquaintances to whom I'd sent that first email.

SPIRITUAL PRACTICES IN ORDER TO HEAR GOD

Over the course of two thousand years of Christian history, fasting has been only one of many spiritual practices that Christians, both as individuals and as communities, have embraced as a way to experience God's guidance and hear God's voice of love. Other spiritual practices that make space for listening to God include:

- consistent attendance at worship
- careful listening to sermons
- many forms of Bible study
- many forms of prayer
- Sabbath keeping
- spiritual direction
- hospitality

The phrase "Christian spiritual practice" is often used interchangeably with "Christian spiritual discipline." In his 1978 landmark book *Celebration of Discipline*,[2] Richard Foster re-introduced the concept of spiritual disciplines to a Western church that had once embraced them enthusiastically but seemed to have largely abandoned them in the twentieth century. In the past twenty to thirty years, numerous books have brought spiritual practices back into focus.

Presbyterian minister Marjorie Thompson, in her 1995 book *Soul Feast: An Invitation to the Christian Spiritual Life*, describes seven spiritual disciplines: reading of Scripture, prayer, worship, fasting, confession/self-examination, spiritual direction, and hospitality. She writes that her purpose is

> to help people of faith understand and begin to practice some of the basic disciplines of the Christian spiritual life. Disciplines are simply practices that train us in faithfulness. . . . Such practices have consistently been experienced as vehicles of God's presence, guidance, and call in the lives of faithful seekers.[3]

Her definition links the vocabulary of "practices" and "disciplines," and draws attention to the fact that any disciple of Jesus needs continued "training in faithfulness" over the entire lifespan.

A second helpful definition comes from Adele Ahlberg Calhoun, a pastor and spiritual director, who describes more than sixty specific spiritual disciplines in her *Spiritual Disciplines Handbook*. Calhoun writes,

> From its beginning, the church linked the desire for more of God to intentional practices, relationships, and experiences that gave people space in their lives to "keep company" with Jesus. These intentional practices, relationships, and experiences we know as *spiritual disciplines*.[4]

Calhoun's definition highlights the fact that if we want to hear someone's voice, we will be more likely to hear that voice if we are "keeping company" with that person.

After Richard Foster's book, individual Christians in Western countries began increasingly to experiment with spiritual practices. As individuals experienced the benefits of those spiritual practices, they talked about those benefits with small groups and whole congregations. As a result, groups of Christians are now discovering the richness of communal participation in various forms of prayer, fasting, meditation on Scripture, and hospitality. My 2012 book, *Joy Together: Spiritual Practices for Your Congregation*, addresses the topic of communal spiritual practices, drawing on dozens of stories from people in congregations and smaller groups who are finding joy in hearing God's voice as they participate in various spiritual practices together. A few of those stories are summarized in this chapter.

When I asked my interviewees where they experienced God speaking to them, they mentioned the Bible, sermons, nature, the voice of friends, and various kinds of prayer. The patterns of communal engagement with the Bible described in the previous chapter are spiritual practices that enable participants to hear God's voice. In addition, many Christians have found spiritual practices such as fasting, praying while walking, and various forms of contemplative prayer helpful in hearing God's voice and receiving guidance from God. We cannot control God's communication with us. We cannot make God speak to us. However, we can make space in our lives so that we are more likely to hear the still, small voice of God when God does speak. We can make ourselves available. We can indicate our willingness to hear and respond. The snapshots in this chapter that illustrate the role of spiritual practices in hearing God speak are by no means exhaustive. But perhaps they will bring to mind additional practices that help you or people you know to receive guidance from God.

COMMUNAL FASTING

Jesus' words in Matthew 6 encourage the person who fasts to put on good clothes and refrain from looking dismal "so that your fasting may be seen not by others but by your Father who is in secret" (v. 18). In the West, those verses have been interpreted to mean that fasting should be done privately, and many of the emails I received when I wrote my book on fasting described attempts to keep fasting private. In Asia, Africa, and Latin America, however, those verses have often been interpreted as a call to avoid pride or arrogance when fasting. As a result of this difference in interpretation, Christians in those parts of the world fast communally and frequently. Fasting is seen as a way to intensify one's prayers and to seek God's guidance individually and as a community. When my husband visited Kenya a few years ago, he was surprised to see that the printed bulletin mentioned the congregational fast day for the month and contained a list of prayer requests for that day. The members of that church fast regularly one day each month as an accepted part of congregational life.

A pastor's wife from South America told me her congregation fasts for a week at the beginning of the year, asking for God's guidance for the congregation's goals and priorities for the following year. Everyone fasts for that week in a way that's appropriate for them. Some people eat no food, people with physically demanding jobs eat a lighter diet, and children are encouraged to give up sweets. She told me about one year when the guidance during the fast was so clear that the congregation knew God was calling them to begin a school.[5]

Similarly, a Presbyterian minister from Zambia told me his congregation fasts every year in January for one day to pray for guidance for the congregation. In addition, he mentioned that fasting plays a role in the ordination process for Presbyterian ministers there. When someone is about to be ordained, all the ministers in the presbytery go on a weekend retreat together, and they take part in a partial fast (fruit and water) all weekend in order to pray intensely for the future ministry of the ordinand. Thus, communal fasting plays a significant role in preparation for ministry.[6]

Although Christians in Africa, Latin America, and Asia have long appreciated the benefits of fasting, *Celebration of Discipline* brought this practice into view for many Western Christians. In the years since Foster's book was published, more individuals and groups have begun to practice fasting, and many of them have experienced spiritual blessings. A friend of mine, the minister of a church in California, told me about a congregational planning meeting on a Sunday after worship. Members were invited to fast from lunch as a way of seeking God's voice and God's presence in the meeting. My friend said the conversation had a sweet spirit to it that had been missing in other similar discussions, and he believes fasting set a particular tone for the meeting.[7]

In many Christian settings, fasting is viewed as an alien and foreign practice. Increasingly, however, people both inside and outside the church are fasting in creative ways, such as technology fasts, setting aside email and Facebook for a specific period of time. These fasts open up space to help us hear God more clearly, and they indicate our willingness to listen.

ADDITIONAL SPIRITUAL PRACTICES THAT INVOLVE THE BODY

For many years, I was a walker. From the earliest days of my Christian life, in my university and early adult years, I loved to walk and think about things. I often prayed as I walked. My mind would wander all over the place, and I viewed my walks as thinking in the presence of God, not as intense, focused prayer. Occasionally, when a specific situation would come to mind, I would pray directly. "God, please help me with this situation." Or "Lord, I'm so concerned about my friend who is sick. Please heal her, and please help the doctors to make the right decisions." Much of the time, though, I was thinking through my life, brainstorming solutions to problems, or toying with ideas about the way various issues were connected to each other, often aware of God's presence with me as I pondered. As a seminary student in my early thirties I wrote an essay about thinking in the presence of God as a form of prayer. I knew that for me, the rhythmic slap-slap of my feet on the sidewalk facilitated that kind of prayer. Writing that essay crystallized for me the significance of that practice.

I was fascinated in the early 2000s to come across a book called *Long Wandering Prayer*. [8] The author, Baptist pastor David Hansen, wrote that so many of us feel like failures in our prayer life, because we think prayer has to be focused and intentional. He wondered if perhaps we place too much emphasis on control and too little emphasis on simply being in the presence of God, pondering the patterns of our lives, something that seems to come easily when walking. Hansen could have been describing my experience. The major difference between Hansen and me is that he found himself praying in a "long wandering" way when he fished as well as when he walked.

I don't think it is an accident that both David Hansen and I could experience long rambling prayer when we did something physical. God made us as integrated beings—heart, soul, mind, and strength—and using our bodies in a rhythmical fashion while being aware of God's presence engages our whole selves. Oddly enough, by the time I read Hansen's book I could no longer go on long walks because of knee pain. I missed those walks deeply. Still, looking back at all those years of walking and praying, I realized that thinking in the presence of God while walking had enabled me to hear God's guidance many times.

Soon after I read Hansen's book, I experienced another form of walking prayer. The setting was a summer session meeting (church board meeting) at the church where I was an associate pastor. The senior pastor, who was moderating the meeting, asked us to walk around the neighborhood in pairs, praying for the people and activities of the neighborhood as we walked. My knees could barely handle twenty minutes of walking, but I wanted to participate. So I paired up with another session member, and we walked slowly and prayed out loud. It felt like a conversation between the two of us and God as we walked. I'll never forget the sense of connection I felt with the neighborhood where the church was located. My prayers for that neighborhood increased in frequency and intensity after that prayer experience on a summer evening.

Another form of prayer that involves the body is walking a labyrinth. A labyrinth is a pattern on a floor or in a garden, and participants often pray as they walk along the pattern. One of the common labyrinth patterns comes from the floor of the cathedral in Chartres, France. In the medieval period, when the floor to the cathedral was laid, making a pilgrimage was a popular form of Christian devotion. For those who couldn't make a pilgrimage, walking the labyrinth in the cathedral symbolized their willingness to view their lives as a pilgrimage with God.

A labyrinth is not a maze, which is a puzzle that requires cognitive analysis. A labyrinth is a winding path that eventually leads to the center, where walkers can spend as much time as they like. Increasingly, churches are building labyrinth patterns into their floors, marking patterns in their gardens using little hedges or paving stones, or painting patterns on a large cloth that can be spread out on the floor of a fellowship hall. This winding path leads to a place of stillness, and it symbolizes the life of faith in a powerful way. It twists and turns like all life journeys. The path takes us to the center, but often we can't see how it's going to get there. These and other metaphors for the life of faith come to mind while walking.

I have walked the labyrinth alone and with others. Alone, walking a labyrinth recaptures some of that "thinking in the presence of God" that I experienced year after year in my walks as a young adult. Walking the labyrinth alone has helped me bring issues that are on my mind into God's presence. Several times I have received clear guidance while walking a labyrinth, and I described one of those instances in chapter 2.

Walking the labyrinth with others is a powerful symbol of the role of community in the life of faith. Sometimes a person who was on the other side of the labyrinth just a moment ago is now right beside you. Sometimes another person's path goes right alongside yours, then your paths diverge. You might walk past someone else several times without ever walking beside them on parallel paths. The center, the place of rest, is where people can be together in stillness. The labyrinth, when walked by people who are already in a community of faith together, can be a place where God speaks clearly and profoundly about the nature of life together.

A few months ago a colleague of mine was ordained as an Anglican priest. As a part of the ordination service, he lay on the floor of the church, face down, in a posture of submission. I envied him that moment of demonstrating with his body his submission to God's call for his life. In somewhat the same way, I often pray with my hands turned up and cupped open to symbolize my desire to receive anything and everything from God. Just the act of turning over my hands changes my heart and makes me more receptive to God's word to me.

Throughout history, Christians have frequently emphasized the soul and ignored the significance of the body. After the Enlightenment and particularly in the second half of the twentieth century, Protestant Christians often viewed faith as intellectual assent to a series of propositions. I wonder what the discussion at a church board meeting would be like if everyone walked the labyrinth together for twenty minutes before the business began, or worked together in a community garden, walked around the neighborhood, or sat for five minutes with their hands turned upwards on their laps as they asked God for guidance and wisdom for the meeting. Just think of the impact on the quality of discussion and listening if everyone lay face down on the floor for a few minutes before a meeting to demonstrate their desire to follow God's guidance as congregational leaders.

CONTEMPLATIVE PRAYER

Contemplative prayer is one more spiritual practice that puts us in a position of receptivity to God's purposes. Chapter 6 presented a number of ways to approach the Bible. Some of those approaches fit within the category of contemplative approaches to the Bible, which include many different ways to ponder, reflect on, or meditate on scripture, alone or with others. All of these practices involve slowing down and moving out of analytical mode into a reflective and receptive space.

I learned several forms of contemplative prayer—*lectio divina, examen*, centering prayer—about twenty years ago during a painful and challenging time in my life. My church held frequent contemplative prayer events, so I learned contemplative prayer forms in community with others. I found the silence and rest of contemplative prayer to be deeply restorative in the midst of the stress of my life at that time. I participated in numerous contemplative prayer groups for several years before I read an article that changed my perspective on the purpose of contemplative prayer. I had been participating in these quiet forms of prayer as a source of peace in the midst of storms. M. Robert Mulholland, Jr.[9] argues that part of the purpose of any kind of prayer is to make ourselves available to God. If we are going to listen for God's voice in any setting, being available to God—in response to God's purposes and priorities—has to be one of the goals of listening.

Mulholland draws on the picture in Revelation 8:3–5 of an angel offering incense, which rises before the throne mingled with the prayers of the saints. Then the angel casts fire onto the earth, and the result is thunder, voices, lightning, and an earthquake. Mulholland argues that this picture illustrates the costliness of prayer. He writes,

> This image also suggests that those whose prayer is true, whose prayer emerges from a life of radical abandonment to God, whose prayer is a life of radical abiding in God, that these persons themselves become the agents of God's presence through a life of radical availability to God. [10]

This idea was astonishing to me and set me on a new path that has shaped much of my writing and teaching about spiritual practices. Yes, we draw near to God because of our own needs for peace, rest, strength, and joy. Those needs are real, and God delights to meet them. However, we also draw near because we are sent into the world as Jesus was sent (John 17:18), and we need the guidance and empowering of the Holy Spirit as we go. Many forms of contemplative prayer can help us receive that guidance and empowering.

The Prayer of *Examen*

Sometimes we don't hear the voice of God because we aren't paying attention to the events of our lives. In the ancient prayer of *examen*, often prayed at the end of the day in monastic communities, we are invited to look back over a period of time to try to discern God's presence and our response to God's presence. After identifying a specific period of time such as a day or a week, this prayer usually has four steps:

- Look for where God was present.
- Respond to that memory of God's presence with a brief prayer, perhaps a prayer of thanks.
- Look for where God was present but I resisted that presence.
- Respond to that memory with a brief prayer, perhaps confession or an expression of intent to do better tomorrow.

I learned *examen* in a contemplative prayer class, and the teacher called this form of prayer "a gentle, unforced noticing." She encouraged participants to look back on our lives gently, not in a rigid, structured way, allowing the Holy Spirit to bring to mind the times when God was present and the times when we resisted that presence. The purpose of the *examen* is to notice, and part of why we don't hear God speaking to us is because we don't take the time to notice the patterns of our lives.

Breath Prayer

When we slow our breathing, many of our other body systems slow down. When we pray with our breath, we tap into that physiological benefit. Many people use a memorized prayer in harmony with their breath, one phrase for each breath. The Lord's Prayer works well, as does the "Jesus Prayer," an ancient prayer based loosely on Jesus' parable about the Pharisee and the tax collector in Luke 18:9–14: "Lord Jesus Christ, Son of God, have mercy on me, a sinner." Another way to use our breath in prayer is to express our needs and concerns to God when we breathe out, and then to use our in-breaths to imagine we are breathing in God's love and care.

Breath prayer works very well in groups. Almost any group benefits from taking a minute to slow down breathing and rest in God. This form of prayer acknowledges our dependence on God for our very breath, a good thing to remember in a meeting as we discuss just about any topic.

Centering Prayer

When most people think of contemplative or silent prayer, they think they will have to spend long blocks of time in silence. The forms of contemplative prayer mentioned above usually involve only short times of silence, perhaps with instructions interspersed. However, centering prayer does indeed involve a long silence. Twenty minutes is often recommended as a good amount of time, but longer times are also common. One form of centering prayer was popularized by Thomas Keating in his many books, such as *Open Mind, Open Heart*.[11] Keating recommends choosing a sacred word, such as a name or attribute of God, to use during the silence as a place to return to over and over. The sacred word becomes a symbol of our willingness to encounter God in this time of silence.

I find it almost impossible to do centering prayer alone for longer than ten minutes. Yet with a group I find twenty or thirty minutes of silence quite comfortable, a rich time of reflecting in the presence of God, a time that encourages abiding and availability. Something different happens in a group, some sort of shared holiness or shared willingness. Some groups spend some time talking about their experience after various forms of silent prayer together, but some groups do not.

SPIRITUAL PRACTICES AND AUTHENTICITY

Numerous other spiritual practices help people hear God's voice individually and communally. In chapter 4, the role of hospitality in one congregation's local outreach ministry was described. While hospitality is increasingly viewed as an important aspect of many forms of ministry, hospitality might not seem to be an obvious candidate for a spiritual practice that makes space for us to hear God. Hospitality, however, opens us to hear the voices of others, and in those voices we often hear God speaking to us. Our perspective is often broadened, and we are more open to the new thing God might be doing.

Thankfulness is another practice that might not come to mind as a way to hear God speak. However, I have experienced over and over that when I stop to notice the things I'm thankful for, I see God's hand in my life in new and fresh ways. For more than twenty years, my husband and I have prayed thankfulness prayers together at least once a week, and that practice has shaped my prayers in other group settings as well. I have led many committees and groups in thankfulness prayers, and I can virtually guarantee that any committee or church group that spends some time thanking God every time they meet will find themselves perceiving God's hand and guidance more often.

To think that we will hear God's voice easily and frequently without making space for God in our lives is one of the myths of our time. The Holy Spirit works in amazing and surprising ways, to be sure, and God's voice does indeed break into our lives in unexpected ways. Yet God's voice is often still and small, and we usually need to slow down in order to hear it. Some people worry that spiritual practices can easily morph into an attempt to prove to God that we are worthy of being loved. Spiritual practices don't help us earn God's approval; they don't impress God or control God's work in our lives. Instead, they open us to receive from God. Spiritual practices make space for hearing God's voice of love and guidance, because they show our desire to listen.

I keep coming across the word "authenticity" as I read about congregational ministry in our time. I read that many young adults long for authenticity in their faith communities, but many Christians in their forties, fifties, and beyond are also talking about their desire for authenticity. Many are saying they desire a pattern of Christian living that is real, honest, and straightforward, without masks or phoniness. Spiritual practices bring authenticity to the journey of faith because they indicate our willingness to listen, to abide, and to be available to whatever God is doing in our situation.

Fasting helps us notice the addictive and absorbing habits of our lives. Fasting communally makes possible rich conversations about those habits and powerful prayers about how to respond. Those conversations and prayers nurture authenticity. Praying using the body in various ways also nurtures authenticity because the body, soul, and spirit are united, and we approach God with our whole selves. Contemplative prayer encourages authenticity because we draw near to God with our inner being. When communities engage in spiritual practices together, the members are able to talk with each other about what they have experienced. This feels real and honest, building trust that God guides and empowers those who open themselves. The spiritual practices mentioned in this chapter, along with many others, help us indicate an inner attitude with our actions, a willingness to listen to God and be transformed.

QUESTIONS FOR REFLECTION, JOURNALING, AND GROUP DISCUSSION

- In what places and times in your life are you most likely to hear God speak or experience God's presence? What habits or practices do you associate with those places and times?
- If a spiritual practice is defined as something we do with some regularity that trains us in faithfulness or that helps us keep company with

Jesus, what spiritual practices are a part of your life? What fruits have you experienced from those practices?

- What spiritual practices are a part of the life of your congregation? In what ways do they make space for God in your life and the lives of others? In what ways do they help you and others hear God's voice? What could you do to nurture and expand your congregation's commitment to the communal spiritual practices that are already a part of your congregation's life?

- Think about your goals in the area of spiritual practices. Write a prayer asking for God's help to meet those goals. Write a prayer for your congregation for its spiritual practices. What do you long to see in your congregation? Include that in your prayer.

- Think about someone who you consider to be authentic, real, honest, and open in his or her faith. This week, pay that person a compliment for what you have observed, and ask which spiritual practices contribute to his or her faith journey.

8

THE LISTENING TOOLBOX

Research indicates many people are poor listeners. Although virtually everyone listens, only a few do it well. Skill in listening is not a "natural ability," but one that everyone must work to develop. Active listening demands concentration. The listener searches for meaning and understanding. It requires energy and effort and is thus potentially tiring because it can be hard work.

—Voncile Smith, "Listening," in *A Handbook of Communication Skills*[1]

I am not a natural listener. I was a talkative child, and in most settings I am still a talkative adult.

My family still chuckles over the humiliating comment on my first grade report card: "Lynne talks more than enough for one." I remember Sunday afternoon car trips in late elementary school. In those days before seatbelts, I would lean forward and spread my arms on the back of the front seat, sticking my head between my parents' heads, and tell them the plot of the latest Nancy Drew book I was reading. In great detail.

I had a best friend in childhood, Wendy, whose loving listening was the anchor of my tumultuous teen years. I wanted to listen to others in the same way that she listened to me. So even as a teenager I began to pay attention to listening skills. In my college years when I learned to lead Bible study groups, I figured out that good listening helps leaders keep discussion flowing. So I continued to work on my listening skills.

In my twenties, someone told me that we remember 90 percent of what we say but only 10 percent of what we hear. I'm not sure those statistics are accurate, but they helped me reflect further on my teaching and leadership strategies. I was motivated to help others learn, so I tried to make space for others to talk, both in group settings and one on one. I tried to learn how to draw people out to enable them to talk about things that matter to them.

In the early 1990s I wrote a murder mystery, *Deadly Murmurs*, with a main character whose listening skills give her information about the murder. I dug the novel out and published it for Kindle as I was working on this book, and as I edited and polished the novel, I realized I was thinking pretty intently about listening skills two decades ago.

About fifteen years ago I was serving as an associate pastor at a church in Seattle, and the personnel committee designed a new staff evaluation process. They gave questionnaires about each staff member to several elders, who were asked to give anonymous feedback by writing short answers to a series of questions. One of the comments about me said this: "When Lynne puts her mind to it, she is a good listener." When I first read those words, I was offended. After all, that comment implies that often I'm not a good listener, that I don't listen well when I'm not focused on listening. Later I realized the comment was a pretty good compliment for someone who has always been talkative. In bits and pieces over many years I have learned listening skills, and when I put my mind to it, I use them well. What more could a talkative person be expected to do?

INTRODUCING LISTENING SKILLS

We often assume that people can listen more deeply if they simply acknowledge that listening matters. Surely that is true to some extent, and I hope the other chapters in this book will nurture a growing commitment to listen. However, learning about specific listening skills can also be very helpful, and fortunately, many of these skills can be described, taught, and developed.

I teach a course on chaplaincy, and half the readings I select focus on listening skills and the significance of listening for chaplains. Last year, after we finished a major module on listening skills, I received comments from two students. Both of them said the readings and discussion about listening skills had been a revelation to them. Before they read and discussed the material, they had no idea that listening skills could be described and taught. One of them told me she had taken some of the readings back to her own congregation and was enthusiastically teaching listening skills to other leaders in the congregation. I hope this chapter will encourage you to do the same.

Listening skills are often put into categories. When we make a commitment to the significance of listening, the first challenge is to learn how to encourage people who are already talking to continue to talk. We do that in many ways, including through body language, nonverbal sounds, words, and silence. We might call these strategies *skills that encourage people to keep talking.* We also initiate and shape conversations, encouraging people to move to topics or directions within a topic that we want to hear about or that we think they should talk about. These might be called *conversational directing skills.*

Two additional sets of skills demonstrate that we are paying attention to the thoughts and emotions of the person we are listening to. One way we express our engagement is through *reflecting* back to people what we have heard. Reflecting gives speakers feedback about what we have heard them say, and when they respond to our reflecting, we get feedback about the effectiveness of our listening. Reflecting can take a variety of forms, but all of them acknowledge the attention we are giving to others' words. Another way we indicate our engagement with the thoughts and feelings of others is through *empathy.* While empathy, closely related to compassion, is not always expressed in words or actions, the degree of empathy we are experiencing influences our ability to use skills that keep people talking, as well as reflecting skills.

All listening skills require a baseline commitment to stop talking ourselves. We simply cannot listen if we are talking. In the past few years, as I have been teaching listening skills to my students and therefore focusing more specifically on what makes listening work, I have been astonished at the number of people who talk 75 percent, 90 percent, or even 99 percent of the time they are conversing with others. If that's you, do some pondering—journaling, praying, talking with a friend—about why it's hard for you to stop talking.

Many obstacles to listening (explored in chapters 9 and 10) impede people's ability to use the skills described here. In the interviews I conducted, I heard about patterns my interviewees observed in congregations and elsewhere. They talked about inner and outer "noise" that impedes listening, and they noted that busyness is a significant obstacle to listen-ing to people and to God. These are big topics that relate to so many aspects of life in the twenty-first century. When teaching listening skills in communities of faith, some reflection on the patterns of life that cause obstacles to listening will be essential, as well as discussion about the ways to create time and energy for listening to people and to God.

SKILLS THAT ENCOURAGE PEOPLE TO KEEP TALKING

A major listening skill involves encouraging people to continue talking. In simple conversations, we might ask, "How are you?" And even if people don't say more than "fine," we can draw them out further if we feel led to do so. In deep conversations, when our conversation partners are sharing significant concerns, sometimes the best thing to do is encour-age them to keep talking, rather than attempting to guide the conversa-tion, simply because people often find within themselves the solutions to their questions or challenges. We can encourage people to keep talking by using a wide variety of skills. Three effective strategies are the use of nonverbal communication, minimal encouragers, and silence.

Nonverbal Communication

Imagine you are talking about a deeply painful situation at work. Your friend is leaning forward, smiling very slightly and watching your eyes, saying nothing but nodding occasionally. When you get to the most pain-ful part of your story, your friend's face reflects your pain, and your friend reaches across and briefly touches your hand. How likely is it that you would keep talking?

Now imagine that your friend is leaning back with a blank expression, sitting with arms crossed, looking behind you at the TV on the wall of the restaurant. Would you continue to talk very long in that situation?

The way we use our body and the expressions on our face are forms of nonverbal communication that can indicate a commitment to listen. Lean-ing forward comes across quite differently from sprawling back. Eye contact, coupled with a pleasant expression, communicates acceptance of what the speaker is saying, while frowning and looking away say some-thing quite different about our attitude. How physically close we are to the person also tells something about our willingness to listen, as do our gestures and our use of touch. Clothing choices can also be viewed as nonverbal communication, a consideration for people in roles such as chaplaincy, where certain forms of dress might be expected.

A sarcastic, strident tone of voice will have quite a different effect on the speaker from a peaceful response. Jumping in very quickly every time the speaker pauses, even to say something encouraging, communicates a hurried attitude, while allowing periods of silence coupled with attentive body language communicates a willingness to listen. A rapid pace of speaking can communicate boredom with what has been said, even if the words are supportive. Tone of voice, pitch, stress, and volume really do make a difference, and it's easy to ignore them, because they aren't verbal.[2]

Nonverbal cues differ from one culture to another. If you desire to develop relationships with people from another culture, check out with them what the nonverbal cues are in their culture that indicate that someone is listening.

Minimal Encouragers

We also indicate our willingness to listen by the short sounds or words we say. "Mmm," "uh-huh," or even a light grunt-like sound can indicate that we are listening. Words and phrases that function as minimal encouragers include:

- Tell me more.
- Oh?
- For instance?
- I see.
- Right.
- Then?
- So?
- I hear you.
- You bet.
- Yes.
- Really?
- Gosh.
- And?
- Go on.
- Sure.
- Darn![3]

People tend to use the same minimal encouragers over and over. I have a friend who uses "okay" repeatedly in conversation. Another friend uses "yes" over and over, and another uses "no way." Recently I've been using "wow" a lot. Monitoring our use of minimal encouragers is essential, because repeated use of the same word or phrase over and over makes us sound like we are listening in a rote fashion like a mechanical doll, rather than with compassion and kindness.

Silence

Keeping silent is often an effective way to encourage people to continue to talk. When choosing to be silent for the purpose of encouraging our conversation partner to keep talking, body language, discussed above, is an important consideration. Our face and our body can vividly communicate our willingness to listen when we're not using words.

Robert Bolton, the president of a consulting firm that teaches communication skills, writes:

> The beginning listener needs to learn the value of silence in freeing the speaker to think, feel and express himself. . . . Most listeners talk too much. They may speak as much or even more than the person trying to talk. Learning the art of silent responsiveness is essential to good listening. After all, another person cannot describe a problem if you are doing all the talking. . . . When an interaction is studded with significant silences and backed by good attending, the results can be impressive.[4]

Bolton uses "attending" to refer to all the ways we indicate we are paying attention, such as body language, facial expression, and nonverbal encouragers. He goes on to explain the many effects of silence in a conversation. For example, silence gives the speaker time to think about what she's going to say next and allows her to set the pace and agenda for the conversation. Periods of silence can be as effective as body language and minimal encouragers in gently nudging the speaker to go further into a topic. Silence can be soothing for someone in any kind of pain, and silence also allows the speaker to express strong emotions such as joy or excitement.

Bolton notes that more than half of the people who come to him for training in communication skills are initially uncomfortable with silence, but he has found that most people are able to increase their comfort with silence relatively easily.[5] If you want to improve your listening skills, consider experimenting with silence. Make yourself listen to someone every day for a few minutes without commenting. Stretch yourself. Notice when it's hardest for you to keep silent, and ponder the reasons why.

If you want to teach listening skills to others, be sure to give them some experience with silences in conversations, perhaps by pairing participants and asking them to take turns listening in silence to each other.

The wise writer of Ecclesiastes notes, "For everything there is a season, and a time for every matter under heaven . . . a time to keep silence, and a time to speak" (verses 1 and 7). Conversations can be diminished by too much or too little silence. Practice is necessary in order to learn to use silence wisely, and the first step for those of us who tend to be talkative is to recognize the value of leaving gaps in conversations.

GUIDING CONVERSATIONS

All listeners guide conversations, steering the speaker toward new topics. We guide speakers in order to get information we need. We guide conversations because we're bored with what the person is saying, and we want to move on to a topic we care about. We can also guide conversations for the benefit of the speaker by drawing them out about the things we think they care most about. One of the major ways we guide conversations is by our use of questions and statements that function like questions. Asking questions also keeps the conversation going, so it is a skill that could perhaps have been included above under "Skills that Encourage People to Keep Talking." Good questions are essential to indicate our interest in what our conversation partner is saying, because without questions, speakers are often unsure whether listeners want them to continue talking. However, asking questions goes beyond encouraging the speaker to keep talking. Questions shape conversations.

Virtually every book on interpersonal communication recommends learning to ask open-ended rather than closed questions. The best way to describe the difference is to say that an open-ended question encourages your conversation partner to say a paragraph, and a closed question encourages him to say one word. Closed questions include any question that would elicit a yes-no answer or any question that asks for a specific piece of information like a time, a date, or a number. "How many sisters do you have?" asks for a word, while "Tell me about your sisters" asks for a paragraph.

Sometimes a closed question will encourage a person to speak, however. Sometimes you need a piece of information in order to proceed with open-ended questions. Sometimes asking a closed question opens a conversation and indicates your interest in the other person. For example, the question, "How many sisters do you have?" could elicit a long answer, perhaps in part because the listener's body language and tone of voice indicate a willingness to hear that long answer. Usually, however, open-ended questions encourage people to talk longer and go deeper, allowing speakers room to go in directions they are interested in. But like all questions, they also allow the listener to guide the conversation, by drawing the speaker in a particular direction. Open-ended questions play a significant role in creating a marvelous give and take.

Questions beginning with "why" seem like they would be great open-ended questions, but often they don't work well. "Why" questions can seem critical or even aggressive. "Why did you make that decision?" can make your conversation partners feel like he or she has been attacked, even if you use a gentle tone of voice. Less threatening ways of asking for the same information include:

- How did you come to that decision?
- What factors led you in that direction?
- Help me understand your process for making that decision.

An aggressive tone of voice can make any question sound invasive, but avoiding "why" helps make questions easier to respond to.

Any statement that begins with "help me understand" is not technically a question, but it functions like a question in a conversation, because it elicits more information and guides the conversation. Other statements that function as questions include statements like these:

- I'd love to hear more about how that happened.
- I'm interested in hearing the reasons for the decision.
- Tell me more about the mission trip.
- Tell me about a typical meeting.
- Explain how you did that.
- Describe it for me.

Questions and statements asking for more information can be overused. Too many questions can make the speaker feel on the spot or even hunted. Some questions that don't communicate compassion and kindness include those that are:

- judgmental or aggressive—"Did you ever consider changing your leadership style?"
- intrusive—"How much rent do you pay?"
- too broad—"What do you think about politics?"
- too numerous—"How many dogs do you have? What kind? What do you feed them? How can you walk that many dogs?"

Effective questions relate to what your conversation partner has said, and they help you find common ground and deepen understanding. Effective questions move the conversation along, perhaps in directions you want to go or perhaps in a direction you sense the speaker is interested in. Effective questions are sensitive and neutral, concrete enough to move the conversation forward while being open and general enough that your conversation partner has options of how to respond. And effective questions use humor at the right moment, making conversations lighter and more enjoyable.[6]

REFLECTING

When we pay attention to our conversation partners' words and body language, and then try to say something that puts into words what they are communicating, we are using the valuable communication skill of reflecting. One of the benefits of reflecting for the listener is that we don't need to think about what we could or should say next. We simply focus on what the other person is saying with their words and their body, and we try to reflect that back in words. Reflecting also helps us listen more accurately, because our conversation partner can correct our perceptions. Four different kinds of reflecting can be used.

- Paraphrasing. When we paraphrase, we listen to speakers' words and try to notice one or two of their sentences that we think addresses their main point. Then we paraphrase their words in our own words, trying to be simple and direct. We can't paraphrase everything that was said because it would take too long, and we would sound like a parrot. Figuring out an important sentence to paraphrase takes a lot of concentration.

- Summarizing. When people discuss a problem, they tend to circle around it, digressing into side issues and returning to the main point several times. Summarizing involves trying to gather up the main ideas and sum them up in a way that the speaker didn't. Summarizing goes one step further than paraphrasing, because the listener is making a judgment about what matters in all the words spoken. Summarizing, like paraphrasing, allows listeners to enable speakers to move forward by helping them crystallize their own thoughts, and summarizing and paraphrasing help listeners express their interest and attention without taking sides or agreeing.

- Drawing implications. Sometimes the listener sees implications that the speaker hasn't perceived yet. Those implications might come from the words spoken or from body language. When drawing implications, the listener is hypothesizing about something that lies behind the speaker's words for the purpose of helping the speaker discover what she was attempting to say.

- Repeating key words and phrases. In some ways this is the easiest form of reflecting. Just pick a word or phrase in what the person said and repeat it back. Often a word or phrase in the last sentence works well. It seems too easy sometimes, but it can be remarkably effective in encouraging the other person to keep talking. However, because it's easy, it can be overused and the listener can begin to sound like a parrot.

An Example of Reflecting

Imagine a setting where your conversation partner is talking about a challenging situation in a neighborhood food pantry sponsored by several churches:

> We have a meeting every month to deal with organizational issues at the food pantry, but we aren't getting strong attendance at the meeting from two of the churches. Then in the week after the meeting, the volunteers from those two churches come to help with food distribution, and they get irritated that procedures have been changed without their input. They're causing conflict among the volunteers, and some volunteers have stopped showing up for their shifts. I think they're avoiding coming here because they don't want to deal with the conflict.

After hearing these words, the listening skill of reflecting could take numerous forms:

- Paraphrasing might sound like this (choosing the last sentence to summarize): "Volunteers seem put off by conflict."
- Summarizing: "There's a pattern of fewer volunteers coming to staff the food bank, and you're concerned that might be because of conflict."
- Drawing implications: "I hear a lot of frustration in your voice," or "You're wondering how to talk to the people at the two churches that aren't sending reps to the meeting."
- Repeating key words or phrases: "Don't want to deal with the conflict," "Avoiding coming here," or even simply, "Conflict."

When reflecting, the listener has to make a decision about what to respond to, evaluating the speaker's emotional state and body language as well as the content of the spoken words. I've given seven possible ways to reflect back after a statement of only a few sentences. Many people speak much longer than a few sentences, and figuring out what to paraphrase, summarize, or repeat, or what implication to state can be challenging.

Making a mistake in reflecting can help the speaker clarify what he really considers to be important or what he really wants to focus on. Therefore, when the speaker says, "No, that's not what I meant," the listener should view that statement as an opportunity to clarify further, not as a failure in listening. Drawing an implication and being wrong can be the listener's gift to the speaker because it helps the speaker clarify his thoughts. Making a mistake in interpretation, and having it corrected by the speaker, can also help the listener understand the speaker's point of view more clearly.

The biggest obstacle with reflecting, however, is the fact that the listener often feels stupid doing it. The words we say as a listener when we are reflecting seem so obvious! How can stating the obvious be helpful to the speaker? When beginning to learn to reflect, simply make yourself do it and watch for the response. Most speakers are delighted that someone is taking their words seriously, and that delight is apparent. Reflecting is a great gift to the speaker, because it gives him the freedom to take his ideas in the direction he wants to go. Reflecting also helps the listener pay attention.

Appropriate and Inappropriate Uses of Reflecting

Reflecting can be overused. If I'm tired, I often restate a word or phrase simply because it's easy. I can tune out a bit while the person is talking and then pick up a word or phrase to repeat and keep them talking. Reflecting, like most listening skills, can be used to avoid genuine dialogue. Most people, however, underuse reflecting because it feels so obvious, awkward, unnecessary, and unproductive, because it doesn't "solve" anything. To encourage you to try it, here's a list of appropriate uses of reflecting:

- to help speakers clarify their thinking
- to clarify your own understanding of what you heard
- to encourage others to talk
- to encourage your conversation partner to direct the flow of conversation
- to keep the conversation focused on the speaker, not on you
- to avoid taking ownership of a problem that is not yours
- to exert some leadership in the conversation by choosing what to reflect[7]

EMPATHY

Many writers on listening believe that empathy is the highest listening skill. We can teach and learn skills related to empathy, but of all the listening skills, empathy is probably the hardest to learn as a skill in itself, because it is so closely related to character. Empathy develops in us as our character develops. Empathy requires some measure of the attributes described in Colossians 3:12 and 13: "As God's chosen ones, holy and beloved, clothe yourselves with compassion, kindness, humility, meekness and patience. Bear with one another." This "clothing," which reflects the character of God as revealed in Jesus, becomes easier to put on as we grow in character and faith.

I have struggled with my weight all of my adult life, and that struggle has been deeply painful. I have talked about those struggles in many settings, longing for encouragement, care, and a listening ear to help me process my shame and discouragement. I've had some outstanding listeners in my life, but all too often listeners have given me advice, moralized about weight, told me that my weight shouldn't matter, or changed the subject.

When I talk about weight, I am usually looking for empathy. A textbook on interpersonal communication defines it like this:

> Empathy is the cognitive process of identifying with or vicariously experiencing the feelings, thoughts, or attitudes of another. Scholars recognize that empathy is an important element in understanding and maintaining good interpersonal relationships. When we empathize, we are attempting to understand and/or experience what another person understands and/or experiences.[8]

The first time I taught the course on chaplaincy where I focus so deeply on listening skills, one of the students argued that empathy is impossible, because no one can fully experience the feelings, thoughts, or attitudes of another. He believed that advocating for empathy is counterproductive and even destructive, because we set people up to fail, encouraging the impossible and giving them delusions about what they can and can't do. My students had a rousing discussion about his ideas. Many of the students agreed that perfect empathy is not possible, but they argued we should still try. Fully experiencing the feelings, thoughts, or attitudes of another can't be done, they said, but trying to experience another person's reality to some extent makes caring relationships possible. I agree that perfect empathy can't be achieved, but I know that partial empathy is a great gift.

Feeling and expressing empathy is easier when we know the person or situation well. Empathy is easier when we have experienced something similar to what the person is describing. The corollary to those two statements is the sad reality that empathy is pretty challenging when we don't know the person or situation very well. Empathy is especially challenging when the interaction crosses cultures or languages. Conversations with people from another culture require a special level of humility, abandoning assumptions that we know how the person is feeling or thinking. Reflecting skills can help us check out our observations.

In most situations, reflecting skills are indispensible for checking to see if we are reading emotions accurately: "You seem pretty angry about this." "I get the sense that you don't feel too upset about this." Using reflecting skills helps us clarify whether we're hearing accurately, and reflecting gives the speaker the opportunity to say more about how they think and feel. All of that builds empathy.

The interpersonal communication textbook that provided a definition of empathy makes several suggestions:

- Make an effort to understand your conversation partners.
- Treat your conversation partners as persons with value, not as objects.
- Pay serious attention to what they are saying.
- Pay serious attention to what they feel about what they're saying.
- Be observant and try to "read" nonverbal behavior.

The textbook authors suggest posing two questions silently as we listen: "What emotions do I believe the person is experiencing right now?" and "What are the cues the person is giving that I am using to draw this conclusion?"[9] They argue that keeping those two questions in mind will help us focus on the nonverbal aspects of the conversation, which is where most people communicate a great deal of emotion.

Empathy alone does not guarantee that the listener will be able to draw out a conversation partner. Empathy can cause the listener to rush into statements expressing compassion, and too many of those statements can shut down a conversation. Empathy can also cause the listener to freeze up or shut down, overwhelmed by the pain expressed by the speaker. Empathetic listening requires the other listening skills in order to be able to act compassionately and appropriately.

An article in *Scientific American*[10] summarized research showing that empathy has decreased over the past three decades. If empathy is the most powerful component of listening, then this research has implications for all of us, including congregations and their leaders. While empathy is probably harder to teach and encourage than other listening skills, the characteristics of empathy can be taught, discussed, and prayed for in our congregations. I believe that over time, the conscious practice of the other listening skills helps develop empathy, because as we discipline ourselves to listen to others, we are nurturing compassion and kindness in our hearts. Therefore, teaching listening skills in congregations and encouraging congregations to be communities that listen will likely increase empathy.

Empathy Enhancers and Blockers

Empathy is enhanced by all the strategies described in this chapter. A posture that indicates we are listening carefully, leaning forward and giving eye contact to our conversation partner, communicates to the speaker and also to our own minds and bodies that we are paying attention. Intentionally using minimal encouragers and periods of silence communicates to the conversation partner and to ourselves that listening matters. Attempting to ask questions that will draw out the speaker and using reflecting skills to check whether we are hearing accurately lets the speaker know we care but also keeps us focused on the speaker, a key posture for empathy. All of these skills draw our minds and bodies into an empathetic posture.

Empathy is blocked by:

- Ordering: "Don't do that again next time."
- Warning: "You'll regret it if you do that."
- Moralizing: "You should be more caring."
- Advising: "Here's what I think you should do."
- Arguing logically: "Let's look at the reasons for that decision."
- Judging: "You really botched that."
- Name calling: "You ministers are all alike."
- Diagnosing: "Your biggest problem is . . . "
- Reassuring: "I'm sure it will work out okay."
- Interrogating: "Why did you do that?"
- Distracting: "Let me tell you about this other thing."[11]

Avoiding those empathy blockers goes a long way to nurturing kindness and compassion in our hearts. Intentions of good will toward others empower empathy, which activates our own emotions as we feel some of the same emotions as the speaker. At the same time, we need to listen with both empathy and detachment; in fact, some degree of objectivity is necessary when trying to be empathetic. We need to pay attention to our own responses as we listen, recognizing that they are indeed our own, so we can avoid the empathy blockers listed above. Emotional detachment, coupled with empathy, helps us figure out effective questions to ask and appropriate ways to paraphrase and summarize what the speaker is saying. Without some level of objectivity, we can leap to wildly inaccurate conclusions about what the person is thinking, feeling, and saying.

CONTRASTS IN LISTENING

A wise listener makes a series of decisions in a conversation. Is this a time to express warm caring or to listen silently? Would I help the speaker most by focusing on the emotions communicated by his body or by paying most attention to the words he's speaking? Would this speaker appreciate my engagement with the facts, details, and possible solutions to the problems she's describing, or would she prefer that I let her talk through options for action without my suggestions? Sometimes a listener has to hold opposing strategies in tension while listening. The four contrasts described here illustrate the role of wisdom in listening. In some settings, one approach works best, and in another setting, a different approach is necessary. Some conversations shift as they flow, and the appropriate style of listening will shift as well. In some conversations, we need to listen in both ways at the same time, or back and forth between one and the other.

Empathetic and Objective Listening

As described above, even the most empathetic conversation needs to have some objective components, some degree of emotional detachment. Discernment is necessary to figure out how much empathy and how much objectivity should be expressed in any given conversation. I'm sure most of us have had the experience of talking about something deeply personal, and the listener immediately goes into an objective analysis of the situation. The listener sees the situation as a problem to be solved, while the speaker desires to receive some emotional support or simply to talk things through, so he can come up with his own solution.

In some settings, however, empathy isn't necessary, and an approach focused on facts, details, and possible solutions is appropriate. When brainstorming about the best way to solve a problem at work or when discussing the garbage and recycling with a housemate, an objective approach focused on the specifics of the situation often works well. In other settings, where emotions or deep thoughts are being shared, a more empathetic approach works better.

Nonjudgmental and Critical Listening

"Holy curiosity" is a wonderful phrase to keep in mind to describe nonjudgmental listening. Holy curiosity encourages us to inquire in a respectful and welcoming way, trying to learn about the other person's thoughts, values, priorities, and feelings. In many ministry settings, and in many caring relationships, a critical approach is not appropriate.

However, problem-solving settings in the workplace, home, neighborhood, or congregation can require critical—analytical and evaluative—listening. Careful assessment is necessary to determine whether nonjudgmental listening or critical listening is more appropriate in any given setting. Some degree of criticism needs to be employed internally in all conversations to analyze the flow of the conversation, to make sure we are using the right listening strategy, and to check to see if we are feeling or expressing any sort of bias as we converse. The challenge is to know when to bring that critical, analytical spirit into the words of the conversation.

Participatory and Passive Listening

Listeners can actively participate in a conversation in many ways, by using attentive body language and minimal encouragers that keep the conversation partner talking, by asking questions that encourage the person to go deeper, and by reflecting back what has been said or implied. Active participation reassures speakers that their concerns and ideas are being received.

I know several people whose listening could usually be described as passive. They listen in the sense that they don't interrupt when I'm talking, and they do not seem eager to turn the conversation back to themselves. These are helpful listening strategies, and I am always so grateful when people don't yank the conversation back to their own concerns. Often passive listening feels to me that it lacks depth, however. Passive listeners give very little feedback that they are hearing anything beyond the surface words I'm saying, so I have no evidence they comprehend or empathize with what I'm saying. Their passivity is confusing, because they seem to be paying attention to my words, but I'm not sure they're engaging with what I'm saying. Using the variety of listening skills described in this chapter helps reassure the speaker that the listener is engaged.

Despite the value of participatory listening in most settings, sometimes passive listening is appropriate. Participatory listening requires a great deal of energy, and sometimes just sitting back and listening without participating conserves energy for other important tasks of the day. Sometimes, when the speaker is moving forward smoothly and clearly, passive listening is the best strategy for encouraging the flow of thoughts and emotions.

Deep versus Surface Listening

Deep listening is wonderful, a true gift, generous and rare. Deep listening requires intense focus and careful deployment of a wide variety of listening skills at the right time to encourage the speaker to go deeper into thoughts, values, and emotions. However, in many casual settings, surface listening is enough. A light discussion about the weather or the latest news item helps people feel connected to each other without going any deeper. A surface conversation about dates, times, and other details is entirely appropriate in many settings.

I notice that I need deep discussions every so often, and I am often surprised where I find them. Someone who is willing to listen deeply gives me a valuable gift. I try to be available to give that gift to others, but I have learned that in many settings people simply don't want that gift, because they are focused on the task at hand. And that's fine, because surface listening is much less draining than deep listening, and no one has the energy to listen deeply in every interaction all day long. [12]

CHOOSING THE BEST TOOLS

I view the skills associated with listening as tools in a toolbox. This toolbox has a variety of tools in it, and the tools are clustered in groups. Unfortunately many of us choose the same tool, or the same cluster of tools, over and over again. We use the same body language to indicate listening; perhaps we always nod as others are talking. We use the same minimal encourager in every conversation; perhaps we always use "okay" to try to show we're listening and we're open to having the person continue to talk. When we try to reflect back to our conversation partners, maybe we always repeat the last sentence they said.

The listening toolbox contains such a variety of skills. What a waste if we don't use them. Overuse of a small collection of listening skills can make our conversation partner feel like we are taking part in a mechanical process rather than an organic and vibrant give-and-take. Some listening skills, such as asking questions—even gentle open-ended questions—are so easy to overuse for the conscious or unconscious purpose of controlling the conversation. The listening toolbox itself can be overused. Some people listen actively and energetically in order to avoid talking, particularly talking about their own lives. Sometimes talking is more appropriate than listening, and we can grow in wisdom about when is "a time to keep silence, and a time to speak" (Ecclesiastes 3:7).

Picking the right tool out of the listening toolbox can be easier if we know the purpose of listening in a particular conversation. Are we listening to get information? To understand issues so we can make a decision? To receive acknowledgment for our own ideas? To empathize? To express appreciation? Paying attention to the goal can help us select the right tools. However, the goal of a conversation can shift rapidly when a new topic, piece of information, or emotion arises. Paying attention to the overall direction of a conversation, as well as the specifics within it, will yield good fruit.

Affirming the significance of listening skills and teaching them in congregations is a wonderful thing to do and a good place to start, but many obstacles to listening impede the use of the skills described in this chapter that make up the listening toolbox. The next two chapters will present a variety of obstacles to listening, and I encourage congregational leaders to ponder these obstacles and discuss them whenever the topic of listening comes up.

QUESTIONS FOR REFLECTION, JOURNALING, AND GROUP DISCUSSION

- As you read this chapter, which listening skills seemed obvious to you? Which skills were surprising or unexpected? Which of the listening skills described in this chapter come easiest for you? Which are hardest? Do you have any theories of why those specific skills are easy or hard?
- If you could work on one of the listening skills in this chapter, which would it be? How would you begin to nurture that skill?
- Which of the listening skills discussed in this chapter do you see manifested most often in your congregation and in the sub-groups within the congregation that you participate in, such as small groups, committees, or other gatherings? Which skills do you see least often? If you could teach listening skills in your congregation, where might that happen?
- Write a prayer for yourself and your listening skills. In your prayer express both your thankfulness for the skills you've already learned and your desire to grow in your ability to listen. In addition, pray for your congregation and the listening skills needed there.
- This week pay someone a compliment for his or her listening skills. Ask that person what were the greatest influences in his or her life that encouraged the development of listening skills.

9

ANXIETY AND LISTENING

More than half of the people who take communication skills training with us are initially uncomfortable with silence. Even a few seconds' pause in a conversation causes many of them to squirm. These people feel so ill at ease with silences that they have a strong inner compulsion to shatter the quiet with questions, advice, or any other sound that will end their discomfort by ending the silence. For these people, the focus of attention is not on the speaker but rather on their own inner disquiet.

—Robert Bolton, "Listening Is More Than Merely Hearing," in *Bridges Not Walls: A Book about Interpersonal Communication*[1]

My father's ability to listen declined with age, and some of the decline had to do with hearing loss. His hearing aids weren't comfortable, so he didn't like to wear them. He simply couldn't hear people very well, so it was hard for him to be motivated to listen.

I'm in a women's writing group, and we meet for lunch before our meeting. The most convenient restaurant is quite noisy, and I find I often don't want to go to the lunches. I generate excuses to skip the lunch, simply because I can't stand the way the background noise makes listening so difficult.

Those experiences illustrate that some obstacles to listening come from the mechanics of hearing, whether that relates to ear function, background noise, or some other issue. Some people speak softly. Some people have accents that make them difficult to understand. Some people speak very quickly, and if there's the slightest background noise or if they lower their volume at all, their words just fly by. As I said in the first chapter, spending some time considering whether people in your congregation's building can hear well will bear good fruit. Sound systems matter. The acoustics in the various rooms of a church building matter. All these obstacles to listening are real and worthy of some creative problem solving. This book, however, does not address those questions. This book focuses on the listening that relates to the interpretation of what we hear.

Many obstacles to accurate interpretation of what we hear come from within. Those obstacles shut down our ability to process the sounds we hear. They impede our engagement with the words, thoughts, and emotions of our conversation partner. These obstacles to listening take many forms. Many of my interviewees talked about the pace of life as a significant obstacle to listening. One of my relatives told me he thinks the primary hurdle to listening is time. Catherine, a Presbyterian minister, talked about the internal noise caused by the pressure of the to-do list. She also noted that fatigue causes internal noise. When we're tired, listening is much more challenging, because listening requires energy. In a fatigued state, we may feel anxious as we converse, because we know we can't do a good job listening, so we quickly turn the conversation in other directions or shut it down.

Stella, a Methodist superintendent, commented on the issue of energy and listening. She remembers a congregation she served as minister where the members were mostly older. "The people only had energy to go from week to week. I tried to put on extra events, things like mid-week prayer and concerts, as a way to invite people from the wider community to come to the church. But the congregation simply had no energy left for listening to what's going on in the inner city." She observed that their energy was stretched to its maximum point by the week-to-week challenges of maintaining a congregation and a building. Listening to the wider community in any form would give these parishioners information about needs, and because they didn't have any energy left over to meet those needs, they found it difficult to hear about them.

Both fatigue and busyness can contribute to anxiety. If I'm feeling tired and the fatigue is impacting my ability to concentrate on what my conversation partner is saying, I might begin to feel anxious. If I'm worried about making it to the next event scheduled for the day, or if I'm thinking about my long to-do list, anxious feelings can simmer inside and shut down my ability to pay attention to the person who is speaking.

Solutions for the impact of fatigue and busyness on listening are not easy to find. Facing these issues can encourage honesty, and discussing them may result in some helpful strategies.

EASY LISTENING?

Like busyness and fatigue, many other obstacles to listening make us feel uneasy and unable to concentrate. One of the listening obstacles that comes from within is described clearly in a communication textbook: "Whenever we feel that our established and cherished beliefs or ideas are threatened by others, we either refuse to listen or our emotions may block and interfere with the process of listening."[2] The textbook authors argue that we need to be aware of our emotional attachment to our beliefs and ideas and realize that others are equally attached to their beliefs and ideas.

One of my close friends, a very good listener, echoed that view. She noted that we are better able to listen if we think we will like what we hear: "It's hard to listen. It's especially hard to listen to things that might be hard to hear." By "hard to hear," she meant painful things that evoke sad, angry, or frustrated feelings, and she was also thinking about things she might not appreciate hearing because they might create a demand that she would have to meet. In chapter 4, I wrote about the Anglican village church that engaged in an intensive listening project. Before the project started, Samuel, the minister there, asked the parish council to take an extra month to pray about whether they were really willing to take part in this project. Recall that Samuel told them, "When you've listened, you can't unhear what you've heard. Be sure you really want to listen and change." Samuel reflected on the process of listening to the wider community about their needs, as well as their views of the church. "We know how out of touch we are in the church, and that raises fear. We don't want to listen to what people think of us, because it would implode our sense of authenticity and who we are. Listening becomes a threat to our identity."

Connie, who led a short-term mission trip to Central America for her church, echoed the same idea. She observed that people prefer to talk with others who are like-minded. "People don't want to have to be transformed. Mission trips are nice things; we go to help and we feel good about helping. But God invites us to be transformed. It's listening that transforms us, the sharing of narrative, the sharing of our stories."

On the mission trip, Connie saw a reluctance to listen that she thought was rooted in fear.

> Fear of having to change the way you buy things, wear things, eat things. Listening to another person's stories blows up the black and white ideas. It makes life more complicated. We prefer to live the lies that make us safe and give us the illusion of control. Listening requires that we be willing to be wrong, willing to be misunderstood, and be willing to have our ideas change. We are afraid that we would be invited to make sacrifices that would be too big, or that if we change, the cost would outweigh the benefits. It takes courage to listen to different opinions.

Listening within a congregation might be less anxiety producing than listening to people in the wider community or people in another culture, but anxiety can arise in any setting. We might feel anxious that we aren't going to be able to understand exactly what the person is saying or that we might not be able to empathize. We might feel anxious because we feel responsible; we believe we need to come up with the right advice, so the situation can be "fixed" quickly and painlessly. We might worry we won't remember what the person is telling us, and we'll be embarrassed later, so we would be better off taking the conversation back into familiar territory now.

Any anxiety reduces our ability to listen, unless we have had some practice coping with it. Later in this chapter, I will lay out methods for coping with anxiety in listening that can be taught to congregation members. The first step is to understand how common anxiety is and to normalize it. Everyone feels it. Every caring listener has to deal with it.

THE DRIVING URGENCY TO TELL OUR OWN STORY

Laura, a therapist and an elder at her church, remembers a situation when she was a young adult. Newly married during the Vietnam War, she and her husband moved across the country to an army base. Laura was eager to make friends on the army base, so she and her husband visited the Officer's Christian Fellowship. She was delighted a few days later when a woman from the fellowship came to visit her in her home. When Laura opened the door, she thought that this might be a first step to making a Christian friend.

The woman sat down in Laura's tiny living room, pulled a booklet out of her purse, and began reading the Four Spiritual Laws,[3] which some people use to summarize the basic principles of the Christian faith. The visitor explained each law, read the Bible verses associated with each one, and when she finished, she got up and left. Laura was incredulous. Minimal conversation, very little chatting, and no questions about Laura's own views about God. "I felt so sad and a bit indignant. Even at the age of 22, I realized we could have had fellowship and shared our situation as Army wives." Looking back on that situation from the vantage point of wisdom gained from many interactions with people, Laura recognized the fear that she believed was driving the other woman. On some level, this woman *needed* to tell Laura the basics of the Gospel to relieve her own anxiety. Laura noted that any internal agitation can impede listening.

> Yet it's self-absorbed to focus on my needs rather than the other's feelings. This can apply to sharing the Gospel. It's messy to listen. It's not black and white. If you know you need to get those Four Spiritual Laws across, it's pretty clear. But listening is less clear. Sometimes listening really does raise our anxiety. We listen to people say off the wall things that we don't agree with, but the point isn't that the truth be spoken. The point is building a relationship. However, this creates a dilemma, because the Bible emphasizes both truth and relationships.

Catherine, the minister mentioned above, wondered if we so badly want to connect through common experience that our listening is inhibited when we come across someone who is talking about something we haven't experienced or that we don't agree with. She talked about "the counterstory that wells up within us" when we are confronted with something that makes us anxious, and she noted that our ability to listen will depend on setting that counterstory aside in order to focus on the person who is talking. Catherine said, "So many people in churches have already come to their own conclusions, and they are willing to listen only to what supports their conclusions. Sometimes we listen well, but usually we go to the places we want to go."

When Laura's visitor talked about the Four Spiritual Laws, Laura experienced someone who had already come to her own conclusions and wasn't willing to have a true conversation, because she evidently didn't want to open the door to anyone else's ideas. That visitor's behavior was perhaps extreme, but every one of us has undoubtedly experienced that "counterstory that wells up within us" as we listen, those moments when someone says something we really don't want to think about, talk about, or deal with because our own inner convictions about the topic are so strong.

One of my interviewees said he has noticed that people ask about the pain in your back, when they really want to talk about the pain in their own back. Our own reality is usually very compelling, and we want to talk about it. Acknowledging that counterstory welling up inside us as we listen to other people talk about their back pain or about their passions and beliefs can help us improve our listening. Paying attention to the anxiety that is raised by the swirling of that counterstory in our brains also helps.

ANXIETY ABOUT THE FUTURE

Many of my interviewees in England talked about fears arising from doubts about the future, whether for the church in general or related to their particular congregation and its chances of survival. I know those fears are very real in many other countries as well, as membership decline accelerates and the culture becomes increasingly secular. Julia, a Methodist denominational leader in the United Kingdom, said:

> We get quite tribal. The Methodist Church has focused on our brand and our badge, and we spend our time worrying about how we can prolong our existence. The danger is that there simply isn't energy for listening to the needs of the wider community in the face of our own needs.

"The church has become a hiding place," another British denominational leader said. "The world out there is frightening and harsh." She agreed that so much energy goes into keeping the church going that there isn't energy left for listening. She believes this is exacerbated by the fact that there are so few places left for people to gather for casual conversation with those who differ in their viewpoints. This absence of gathering places leaves church people in their own enclave, working hard to keep their congregation alive but with little contact with outsiders.

Jane, a theological college lecturer in England, has observed fear among Christians. "You have to get out amongst people in the wider community with an openness. We're scared we might lose control. We're also scared because we don't have a lot of resources. We seem to think we've got to do it all tomorrow and on our own." She went on to talk about the fact that these fears impede listening, in part because they create a sense of failure and doom.

Kate, a curate in an Anglican church near London, has also observed significant fears about resources. She believes that much of this fear is rooted in a theology of scarcity. She has observed that this theology of scarcity impedes listening to other people's visions, because we can't see that they might themselves be resources and available to participate with us in what God is calling us to do. Instead, when we hear about needs, all we can see is a lack of resources, which raises anxiety, and therefore effective listening stops.

Kate noted that if someone in a congregation dreams up a project, the immediate response is usually, "If we do this project, how will it be resourced?" Another common response is, "It won't work," based on previous attempts to do something similar, even if the situation was quite different or a very long time ago. The weight of tiredness and weariness is very real. Kate often hears the words, "I'm an old timer," coupled with statements about not being able or willing to face any more changes. Kate wonders if those words imply that we've got to wait until everyone dies to start afresh.

The Church of England has a particular challenge in its old buildings, Kate said. "Lots of listening is directed toward issues related to maintenance of our buildings. We have massive buildings to maintain, and we're stuck there." She said many church buildings have become a ball and chain for their congregations. Kate was adamant when she said, "I keep coming back to the story of scarcity, which I believe is a lie being peddled. It's insidious and undermines everything. What we need is to retell the story of abundance." Understanding the abundance of the Gospel, she believes, will help congregation members to find courage to look beyond themselves and look for resources that may be more available than they think. A theology of abundance will help people listen more openly.

ANXIETY ABOUT BEING REJECTED OR NOT HAVING ANSWERS

Kate noted that many of the people in her congregation are unwilling to go door to door in their neighborhoods, even to deliver an invitation to an event. They are scared of the prospect of knocking on someone's door if they don't know that person, and sometimes even if they do.

Hannah, a United Reformed Church seminarian in England, said that she has observed that most people are uncomfortable talking to someone they don't know. "So people talk to the people they're used to talking to." Despite this pattern, Hannah notes that many people in churches consider themselves to be friendly and welcoming, and therefore believe they don't need encouragement or training in talking to people they don't know. Hannah remembers an amusing interchange at a congregational meeting to discuss how the small congregation might become more welcoming to new people. Congregation members stayed after church for the meeting, and the general tone of the discussion was "Yes, we're welcoming; we're very friendly already." One man who had been there only two Sundays had decided to stay for the meeting. He spoke up somewhat diffidently in the discussion to say only two people had talked to him in the two times he had attended church there. The response from a congregation member was, "Two! That's good."

Several of my British interviewees said that many people in England have been brought up to believe that religion is a private affair, so religion is something you simply don't probe into in a conversation. Therefore, deep discussion about faith issues is sometimes difficult even in Christian congregations. But this privacy about religion has other implications as well. It makes it difficult for many people, not just British people, to talk about religion with people outside the church. Since religion is such a significant component of culture, asking questions about the values or culture of Hindu, Buddhist, or Muslim neighbors seems invasive, because the topic of religion might come up. And the topic of religion often raises the listener's anxiety, so those conversations are avoided.

Jacob, a retired school chaplain, believes that in congregations and settings outside congregations, people are unwilling to listen because often they don't know how to. In addition, he believes many people don't dare go further and deeper in conversations because questions might be raised that they don't know how to answer. He has observed that Christians are very afraid of the "where is God in the tsunami?" questions. People are afraid they won't have answers to the deep questions people have about God, so discussing those questions might do harm to both the speaker and the listener. Jacob would like to see ministers address those "so called ultimate questions" in sermons more often in order to give congregation members confidence that even if we don't have complete answers to those questions, "we can give sufficient direction to make us worthy of being listeners."

He said others are in awe of him that he can converse with people from so many different backgrounds about faith issues in the midst of crises, which often raise deep questions about God's love and God's power. "I don't know how you can take it. I couldn't handle it," they say to him. Jacob said that he can handle it in part because he knows he can't solve other people's problems, and he knows he can't answer all the questions he hears. "I can handle it because I know they're getting something out, which won't hurt me." And discussing those issues might even help the person who is talking. At the very least, a connection between the two people has usually deepened.

Many of my interviewees believe that a central task for congregations today is to equip members to talk about their faith more naturally and more easily. Several interviewees observed that church people are readily listening to the wider media and the wider culture, which so often present the conviction that God and the church are irrelevant and that no intelligent person would want to discuss those issues. Yet significant interest in spirituality and questions about the meaning of life can be observed in popular TV shows, movies, and novels. Equipping congregation members to feel more comfortable talking about issues of God and faith requires affirmation that many more people are interested in spiritual issues than are visible in the news media. An affirmation that we don't need to have all the answers in order to converse on a topic, that listening in and of itself shows love, can also reduce anxiety. Gaining confidence in listening skills can play a role in equipping Christians to converse with people in many walks of life about "ultimate questions." Confidence that people often do want to talk about spiritual issues, and that we don't have to have all the answers as we listen, can lessen anxiety.

LEARNING TO DEAL WITH ANXIETY

Anxiety while listening is largely unavoidable, but some causes of anxiety can be lessened by acquiring skills. When we become skilled in asking effective questions and reflecting back what we have heard, we realize that we don't have to have all the answers or remember everything a speaker has said, so we can relax into the conversation. Confidence with listening skills helps us see that often the biggest gift we can give is our care and focus on our conversation partner's thoughts and feelings.

However, even with good listening skills, anxiety is a given in many conversations. I cannot imagine that even the most laid-back, easygoing person is completely free from anxiety in every conversation. Surely all of us have experienced those moments when something inside of us whispers—or screams—"no" when someone is contradicting one of our deeply held values. Surely all of us have felt at least some degree of tension when we want to listen deeply, but we simply can't do that because of a looming appointment or too many things on the to-do list. Surely we have all been concerned that we're not getting someone's story straight when we are tired or overwhelmed.

This anxiety can be managed, and it must be managed in order for us to focus as fully as possible on our conversation partners, rather than on our own need to have our anxiety relieved. Learning how to deal with the anxiety that so often arises in us when we listen is a major listening skill, one that can be practiced just like other skills. It is a skill that improves as we practice it. Yet this significant listening skill, perhaps the most significant listening skill, is rarely talked about.

Acknowledge It

The first step in developing the skill of coping with anxiety while listening is to acknowledge it exists and that it is common. Feeling a bit tense in listening situations does not indicate that something is wrong with the listener, that we aren't loving, or don't have good listening skills. Anxiety is simply a component of many conversations, and affirming that reality can free people from unnecessary self-condemnation and self-criticism. Whenever listening skills are taught or even mentioned, the teacher, leader, or preacher can highlight this central truth. Most people feel anxious sometimes in conversations.

Usually the listener internally acknowledges her anxiety, and the conversation partner never becomes aware of the anxiety the listener is experiencing. However, sometimes it's appropriate to acknowledge the anxiety in the conversation by saying something like, "I'm feeling anxious about getting to my doctor's appointment on time, so I need to cut this conversation short. I'm sorry I can't listen to you very well right now."

Set It Aside

The second step involves figuring out ways, after acknowledging the anxiety, to set it aside. This process is sometimes called "double listening" and involves paying attention to our conversation partner while recognizing our own inner state and responding appropriately to both. A healthy response to anxiety is to acknowledge it, then set it aside for the duration of the conversation.

One analogy that many people have found helpful is to imagine parking the anxiety somewhere during the conversation, perhaps on the distant side of a parking lot or beside a beautiful stream. Perhaps I feel anxious several times during a conversation, so my anxiety parking lot may have a number of cars in it by the end of the conversation. Sometimes acknowledging the emotion inwardly in my own mind and choosing to set it aside makes it dissipate. Sometimes the emotion will still be there, parked to the side, when the conversation ends, and I might want to examine it through journaling, talking with a friend or family member, or praying about it, pondering why the anxiety arose and what it might be teaching me.[4] Whether or not I need to deal with the anxiety at the end of the conversation, parking it during the conversation can prevent it from interfering with my listening.

Occasionally acknowledging what we are thinking or feeling in the conversation works well if the time is right. "I get really tense when you talk about that, but I do want to listen to what you have to say. So if I seem anxious, just keep talking." This is particularly true in conversations between friends and family members where intimacy has been developed and the caring goes both ways. However, in many conversations, our central task is to learn to set aside our anxiety for the moment in order to listen.

Remember that I'm Not Responsible

A lot of anxiety in listening is caused by the belief that I need to fix my conversation partner's problem. That anxiety often manifests itself in offering advice or pat answers, which will be discussed more fully in the next chapter. Loving listeners know they are not responsible for the other person's life. Sometimes we are called to help meet a need, but the person who has the problem usually needs to come up with the solution or participate in the solution.

One way to move the anxiety into the parking lot when hearing about someone else's pain is to remind ourselves that their problem is simply not ours to fix. Sometimes a brief internal prayer while listening, entrusting the person's problems into God's hands, helps us remember we are not responsible. Occasionally I say in a conversation, "Oh, how I wish I had a magic wand that would solve this problem you're describing. I feel so sad about this." Sometimes saying words internally to ourselves can help as we listen and are tempted to feel responsible, something like, "How I wish I could fix this, but I'm not God, and I can't fix other people's lives."

Remember I Don't Have to Have the Answers

Much anxiety during listening is driven by the conviction that I as a listener should have answers for life's problems. Can I view myself as a competent person if I can't think of solutions to the problems I'm hearing? Does my faith in God have any value if it doesn't provide answers to the kinds of questions my conversation partner is raising? The conviction that I should have answers flows out of an overly simplistic view of life and God's power in the world, as well as a lack of understanding of the brokenness in the world and the power of sin. However, many forces in society and in the church nudge us to believe that answers should be easy and straightforward, so I often find myself falling for the myth that I should be able to think of answers for my conversation partners. Relinquishing this myth is essential in becoming a good listener.

Assure Myself that I Don't Have to Remember or Understand Everything

Some anxiety arises from the fear that I'm not going to catch everything the person says. Remembering what someone has told us communicates love in a powerful way. What if I can't remember? Won't my listening partner feel unloved? As listeners, we don't have to worry. Most people circle around issues and repeat themselves quite a bit. Usually, an opportunity will arise to catch the main points again. And if not, we can always ask questions. Most of the time, people don't mind repeating things that matter to them.

Our fears about remembering and understanding are one more form of anxiety that needs to be parked somewhere. No one can remember everything. No one can understand all the issues a friend, colleague, or acquaintance is addressing. We can only do our best, and our best in any given moment involves setting aside our own fears and giving our attention to the person we are listening to.

Keep in Mind that I Don't Have to Agree

One of my interviewees said, "We have to be willing to be changed. That's why we find it so hard to listen. It's hard for us to want to change." The theme of being willing to be changed came up in many of the interviews. What kind of change is required by listening?

Effective listening requires that we grow in understanding, not that we have to change our values or priorities to match the other person's. This distinction is easy to misunderstand. Many people seem to believe that if they were to listen to someone from a different faith tradition or someone who holds different political values, their own commitments would be called into question, and they would automatically be forced to change, to agree with the person they are listening to.

Certainly, sometimes the understanding that grows from listening will enable us to change our priorities or values. But when we say, "We have to be willing to be changed," the change we are embracing begins with understanding. This growth in understanding is often the full extent of the transformation we are being called to. Listening helps us understand the motivations, priorities, passions, and values of another person, which increases empathy and love, so, yes, we do change by leaving behind our blind judgments and extreme criticisms, so we can grow in understanding. However, we can understand people without agreeing with them. We can love people without agreeing with them. This distinction relieves a lot of anxiety.

FACING INTO ANXIETY

The Enneagram is a model of human personality that focuses on the deep central motivations we all have.[5] Of the nine interconnected Enneagram types, one of them has a significant component of anxiety. People of this personality type—called the Six—are deeply motivated to feel safe and secure, and to avoid anxiety at all costs.

When I've led seminars about Enneagram types with church groups, several times participants have remarked that they seem to have a lot of Type Sixes in their churches. These participants have commented that a drive for security and freedom from anxiety causes many church people to resist change, because change feels threatening. Whether or not you are interested in Enneagram type, look around your congregation and ponder the ways that a drive for security plays a role in congregational conversations and decision making. When congregation members or lay leaders resist change, can you detect in their words a drive for security and familiarity?

As someone who is passionate about the value of learning listening skills, I find myself wondering if learning the listening skills described in chapter 8 and in this chapter might help people who have a deep drive to feel secure. I wonder if these skills might help lighten some of the load of anxiety that many people feel when they talk with others. Acknowledging how common anxiety is when listening might encourage a willingness to talk about difficult topics and give us comfort and security when doing so. I am optimistic that acknowledging that all listeners feel anxiety can bring freedom from self-criticism. I hope that the analogy of parking anxiety to one side will provide a skill and strategy that can help lower the level of stress while listening. Remembering that I'm not responsible for fixing people's problems, that I don't have to have all the answers, that I don't have to remember and understand everything, and that I don't have to agree in order to be a good listener will, I hope, ease the challenge of listening. The next chapter will focus on some of the other internal realities that affect listening, including the need to be right and to solve others' problems. As we have seen in this chapter, anxiety plays a role in those thoughts and feelings as well.

QUESTIONS FOR REFLECTION, JOURNALING, AND GROUP DISCUSSION

- Describe some of the settings where you are most likely to feel anxious as a listener. What strategies are you already using to reduce anxiety in those settings? What strategies might you try?
- Think about some of the effective and ineffective listeners in your life. What role do you think anxiety plays in their listening patterns?
- Ponder your congregational culture. Do you see members or leaders embracing beliefs or values that might be making them more anxious as listeners? In what settings might leaders or members discuss strategies to reduce anxiety as listeners?
- What beliefs and attitudes toward evangelism are common in your faith tradition? What role does listening play in your tradition's view of evangelism? What role might it play?
- Write a prayer for yourself on the subject of anxiety and listening, expressing to God what you hope for and long for. Write a prayer for your congregation and its leaders related to the kinds of anxiety that shut down listening.
- Think of someone you know who appears to be a calm listener, not easily disturbed by a conversation partner's emotions or opinions. Pay that person a compliment, and ask him or her what factors enable calmness while listening.

10

HUMILITY AND LISTENING

There are many causes of ineffective listening and all of us are guilty of some of them at some time. In fact, it is almost impossible to maintain a high involvement in listening all the time. We need to "tune out" to give our minds a chance to rest, but we also need to be able to "tune in" when we want communication to succeed.

—Terry Mohan, Helen McGregor, Shirley Saunders, and Ray Archee, *Communicating! Theory and Practice*[1]

Alison is a Presbyterian minister who has worked much of her career as a hospital chaplain. She described several obstacles to listening, beginning with the urge to be efficient and productive:

Listening is not time efficient. Meetings at churches have deadlines. Maybe we need to map out a Sunday school curriculum today, but if God isn't speaking today, we still need to decide. If we put off the decision because we don't hear God's voice today, we would have to meet again, and the youth director is just about to leave on vacation.

She also noted that good listening requires an inner self-discipline that keeps distracting thoughts and emotions from impeding the listening process. "If you're really listening, you can't be always thinking about what you'll say next. That's hard, and it requires deep restraint. And if you're listening for God, you need to focus on listening, not on preparing your response." This kind of self-control is difficult to achieve and requires a level of commitment and concentration that is hard to find in our busy, active congregational cultures.

Alison noted another necessary attitude. "Listening requires a posture of humility that isn't 'sexy.' If you're really going to hear God and others, you have to be open to not being right and to seeing something new. But you can't hear God and others if you don't have that attitude in some measure."

She said countless brochures for conferences and speakers come across her desk, and she's never seen a single one that focuses on humility. Humility, she noted, is not a trend. "I don't see church leaders being fired up about humility. There are no big conferences, no programs. What's 'sexy' now is emergent church and programs that promise quick results. Being humble isn't an obvious thing and you don't get any kudos for it." Several inner convictions and attitudes make humility in listening more difficult to achieve, including thinking we already know answers and loving action and activity.

WE THINK WE ALREADY KNOW

In the chapters on listening in congregations and listening to the wider community, I described some of the implications of thinking we already know what people will say. We stop listening, or we don't ask questions to draw people out, because we think we know what we will hear. Several interviewees talked about this obstacle to listening. A youth worker said, "You think you know what someone thinks. Even if they're talking, you can find yourself not listening because you assume you know." A retired United Reformed Church minister attributed this listening obstacle to a lack of imagination. He cited Jesus' healing miracles where Jesus enabled blind people to see and deaf people to hear. After the miracles, they were able to see and hear things they hadn't previously perceived. He believes we need to cultivate a willingness to see and hear things we haven't previously seen and heard.

A Presbyterian minister believes it takes practice to cultivate an openness to hearing what we think we already know. In addition we need to strive for a wide focus rather than a narrow view. "Three-quarters of it relates to being willing to see what's there, and 25 percent comes from skills. The challenge is to learn to see what's there rather than our preconceived notions of what we're seeing." Her emphasis on attitude, practice, and skills indicates that the more often we listen with an open stance, the easier it becomes.

With respect to listening to people in the wider community, many people of faith listen to the media to get information about what people outside the church are thinking. Daniel, a theological college lecturer who teaches evangelism. noted:

> The media tells us Christianity is irrelevant or that this is a secular nation. We don't listen to individuals who would have their own stories and perspectives. Because of what we hear in the media, we assume we know what people outside the church believe and think. As a result, churches become their own bubble. They think they know what people outside need.

The need for listening to individuals rather than lumping people into groups came up in an interview with Anna, the minister at a small Presbyterian church. In part because of the size of her church, she enjoys connections with ministers from other churches. Her presbytery is quite divided over issues of sexuality, and Anna mourns the divisions and resulting lack of listening. She calls it "the labeling thing. Once we label people, we believe we already know what they're going to say. We know who's to the right and left of us, and we stop listening."

A new minister came to Anna's presbytery, and Anna made a conscious choice to befriend her, even though she knew from the woman's seminary background they would be poles apart on their theological perspective. Anna described her pleasure in the relationship:

> We're really enjoying each other. There's a sweetness to conversations that don't focus on battle positions. I love talking with people who have different theological perspectives about their summer vacations. What does it mean to lay down our issues and move on? We're failing in the wider church to listen to each other well. It's our central failing right now.

Humility is necessary in order to listen when we suspect we already know what the other person will say. Humility is necessary to lay aside battle positions with someone we know we disagree with in order to listen to an account of a summer vacation. Humility is necessary to set aside what we think we know based on media accounts of what people outside the church think in order to listen to a specific individual's beliefs, priorities, and feelings.

WE LOVE ACTION, STRATEGY, AND KNOWING THE ANSWERS

Another obstacle related to humility is our love of getting things done, of strategy, and of planning. Anna, like Alison from the beginning of the chapter, noted that she gets so many books and flyers that advocate specific programs. "'Follow these ten steps,' they all seem to be saying. That's our model for growth, not listening to God or listening to each other."

A children's ministries director noted,

> We want to be busy. It goes against the grain to slow down and create space for God to work. We've been trained that we've got a lot to do, so let's get to it. In children's and youth ministries, there's so much pressure to keep functioning. All the programs are so valued. You have to have something every Sunday.

She believes an obstacle to listening to God and to others is the fear that I might have to change my plans. "What if God wants me to do something I don't want to do? What if God nixes something I want to do?"

A denominational executive noted that he tries to slow down, listen well, and honor the people present. "But I'm really good at strategy! My immediate response in most situations is to say, 'Let's put good ideas together and strategize!'" He recognizes that inner tension in himself, his love of action and planning. To slow down and listen requires a conscious commitment.

He talked about the eagerness to rush through congregational transitions, which he has observed in many leaders. That in-between space is challenging, so moving ahead with plans relieves the anxiety of the unknown. He remembers attending a meeting at a congregation in transition, and he could hear two sets of voices. Some people wanted to rush into rapid planning, and others wanted to slow down, let things settle, and listen to God and to each other. The people who wanted to move on quickly won the day, probably because their anxiety was high, so they put a lot of energy into expressing their opinions.

He reflected on the challenge of slowing down to listen. "Openness to hearing what you don't anticipate is hard. Often you feel fearful of discovering something you don't know what to do with. We want solutions, and some people think if they can't solve it, they've failed." So we rush into action. Waiting and listening is just too hard. Being active shows we're doing something, and doing *something* makes us feel good about ourselves.

Julia, a Methodist denominational leader, expressed similar thoughts:

> I think human beings in general are better at reacting than reflecting. We want to fix problems, and the danger is that we rush to attend to symptoms rather than underlying causes. In my experience, without training in reflection people find it hard to reflect on their motivations and this can lead to ill-considered responses. Moreover, under pressure, human beings tend towards firefighting rather than planning what to attend to and what to neglect. To listen to God requires stopping some things. A decision not to make a decision is a decision, and it can be an honorable decision that acknowledges that we don't yet know the will of God.

Julia expressed some of the same reservations about voting in congregational decision making that were expressed in chapter 5. She would like to see an increased emphasis on deep listening to increase understanding of how others view situations.

Julia noted that many Christians come from a church background that affirms "There is an answer and their job is to absorb the answer. It's all about a cognitive scheme." Instead, she advocates a focus on listening and understanding others' viewpoints. Her comment ties back to the anxiety issues described in the previous chapter. If church has always been a place where answers are clear and straightforward, then stopping to listen to the mess of ideas that people have can raise anxiety, because clarity is hard to find. And listening to God in that context is difficult as well, because God doesn't always speak clearly to individuals or to groups.

This drive toward self-justification by keeping busy has significant implications for humility. Humility and its synonyms—modesty, meekness, humbleness, lowliness, unpretentiousness, and the absence of arrogance—have long been valued in Christian tradition. Many Christian writers throughout the centuries have described Jesus as exemplifying these qualities. In contemporary Christian congregations in Western countries, humility is still valued to some extent, but action and productivity are valued more highly. Because the world is changing so rapidly and congregations are impacted so profoundly by those changes, we need to slow down, pay attention, and listen for God's guidance. We need to realize we don't have all the answers, and that's okay. We need to rediscover modesty and meekness. We need to be willing to work hard to hear and follow God's guidance.

The value placed on action and the drive to keep busy can result in a kind of pride and self-justification that completely undermine God's grace. My favorite definition of grace comes from the well-known words of Philip Yancey: "Grace means there is nothing we can do to make God love us more. . . . And grace means there is nothing we can do to make God love us less."[2] As long as we cannot stop functioning, as long as we cannot pause and reflect and listen, we will always be in danger of believing that our actions matter more than God's love, which so often comes to us through other people. Rediscovering humility about God's abundant gift of grace to us can help us listen better, and listening better can help us rest in grace in a humble spirit. Growing in understanding and living into grace can also help us get a grip on what exactly humility is.

TRUE AND FALSE HUMILITY

Historically, Christians have warned against two vices related to humility: false humility and pride. True humility involves avoiding those two opposite pitfalls. False humility or an excess of humility often results in an inability to serve God well because of an overly low view of the self and one's gifts for service. An excess of humility can also lead to obsequiousness, excessive flattery, or co-dependent submission to others. This characteristic is sadly present in communities of faith when some individuals don't think they have anything to contribute and are in awe of those who do contribute. False humility is often not just present in communities of faith, but also encouraged and validated.

I have a hunch that pride, the other vice related to humility, is also quite common in congregations, but it is usually masked. One of the masks is activity. As several interviewees noted above, a knee-jerk response in the midst of a problem or crisis is to do something, because it helps us feel better about ourselves. We love solving problems. The denominational official quoted above said, "I'm really good at strategy! My immediate response in most situations is to say, 'Let's put good ideas together and strategize!'" We like to do what we're good at, and many of us are good at planning and action.

Another mask for pride is spiritual certitude. We think we know what the Bible says, what's right and wrong, and what people inside and outside the church need. We know, therefore we don't need to learn more. In order to speak God's love and truth into this hurting world, we need greater understanding of what's going on in people's lives. We need the kind of humility that helps us know we always have something to learn.

One kind of listening that looks humble might be called pretend humility. Listeners sometimes say "I hear you," "good idea," or other affirmations when they are not taking in what the speaker is saying and have no interest in taking anything they hear seriously. Pretend humility can sometimes be identified by a paternalistic tone of voice, or by the fact that the platitude isn't followed with any further comment or action. Sometimes pretend humility is quite confusing, because the speaker thinks the message has been received, while in reality the words are completely ignored.

Almost everyone has times when they feel they need to be right, need to be in control, and want to show competence. Almost everyone has moments when all they can summon up is a platitude in response to words they have no intention of taking seriously. We saw in the previous chapter that almost everyone has times when they feel anxious in conversations. We might feel anxious about the to-do list spinning around in our head or about the lunch we need to prepare in just a few minutes. We might feel stressed trying to find a moment in the flow of words to express our opinion or to ask an urgent question. We might long to fix another person's painful problem, even though we know we can't, and our deep concern for the other person and our inability to change their life for them creates tension in us.

What are the characteristics of listening when we have these emotions roiling around inside and we are unable to park them somewhere outside the conversation? In those times when we need to be right and want to be in control, in those times when we feel anxious, listening deeply does not come easily. We commonly stop listening in those situations.

AN EXAMPLE OF ROADBLOCKS TO LISTENING

If we are unable to set aside our own inner reality and focus humbly on the other person as we listen, we are likely to jump into one of four patterns—solution giving, judging, denying, and interrogating—that meet the needs of the listener, not the speaker. Using these roadblocks, most often unconsciously but sometimes on purpose, reduces the listener's anxiety and elevates the feeling of being competent or in control.

Imagine this scenario. The parish council has received a complaint from Mary, a congregation member and children's ministries leader, about the ex-offender support group that uses the church building on Thursday evenings. Sandra, one of the parish council members who is entirely supportive of having former prisoners meet in the church building, has volunteered to meet with Mary to talk further. In the conversation, Sandra finds that Mary usually comes to the church building to organize the children's supplies and make lesson plans for Sunday school at the same time the ex-offender support group meets there, and Mary sometimes feels afraid when she encounters group members in the hallway.

As Sandra listens to Mary talk about her fear, a variety of thoughts run through Sandra's mind. She realizes she has never felt a moment of fear when she encounters former prisoners in the hallway, so she wonders what makes Mary so timid. Sandra also acknowledges that even though she is a can-do person, confident in her ability to solve problems, her sense of competence is wavering a bit, because she is a fairly new member of the parish council, and she feels some anxiety about her skills in a congregational leadership role. Sandra makes several attempts to guide the conversation in a way that will relieve her anxiety and show she's competent.

Offering Solutions

Sandra immediately suggests, "Why don't you come to the church building at another time to organize the children's supplies?" Mary replies that Thursday evenings work best for her, because her workday on Thursday is shorter than on other days. Sandra then brainstorms other solutions. "Could you time your arrival so the meeting is already going on?" Mary says she's tried that, but the people in the support group often go down the hall to use the bathrooms, and she needs to move around in the hall in order to gather supplies. "Could you come earlier to gather the supplies, before the group meets, and then finish your lesson planning in the children's room, with the door locked? Do you have a key to lock the door to the children's room from the inside? I could get you one."

Giving solutions often leaves people feeling misunderstood and judged. Mary's not stupid. She has been trying to come up with a resolution to the problem herself. Jumping into solution giving relieves the anxiety of the listener, because solution giving encourages us to believe there is an easy way to solve every problem and that we're smart enough to figure it out. Humility would be necessary in order for Sandra to say, "I bet you've tried some solutions. Maybe you could tell me what you've tried. Then maybe we brainstorm together some ways to adapt the things you've tried or come up with some more ideas." Humility might also help Sandra say, after she made all the proposals described above, "Wow, I really missed the boat with those suggestions. You've thought of them and more. What do you think are the next steps you and I—or the parish council—should consider next?"

Solution giving taps into our need to take action, to be practical and strategize. Perhaps the most effective way for Sandra to begin would be to say, "Tell me about how the situation with the ex-offender support group has affected you. What are your greatest concerns?" In order to do that, Sandra would need to let go of her need to act and solve the problem.

Judging

After coming up with a series of solutions that Mary deflects because she has already tried them or already knows they won't work, Sandra might be feeling that Mary is a bit stubborn. And from the beginning of the conversation, Sandra has been thinking Mary is hypersensitive. Sandra might refrain from expressing those judgments, but they may very well come across through her body language and facial expression. Or Sandra might try to express her perceptions: "Surely you could come up with something!" or "Don't you think you're overly sensitive to the possibility of danger?"

Humility is necessary in order to acknowledge that our inner judgments might be wrong, and humility helps us refrain from expressing the judgments we're thinking about. Judgments often arise from anxiety. In

Sandra's case, they might arise from her fear that Mary's concerns will impact the church board's willingness to let the ex-offender group continue to use the building, from her underlying anxiety that she's not competent to sit on the parish council because she's not able to solve Mary's problem easily, or from nagging thoughts about her own fears in some settings. Thus, judgments often help us deflect our fear that we might have some of the same weaknesses or uncontrollable emotions that our conversation partner seems to have. Consciously choosing to face, and then set aside, our anxiety can reduce the tendency to leap to judgments.

Denying

Listeners sometimes use praise as a way to deny a problem exists. Sandra might say, "You've done such a great job with the children's ministries, I'm sure you'll figure out this problem." Reassuring is another denial strategy. "I'm sure it will be fine. I've never heard of any danger from the ex-offender crowd." Distracting and changing the subject also denies the significance of the problem. Sandra might dive into a conversation about a new project the church board has in mind, hoping to get Mary's mind off her discomfort.

Denial strategies get the listener off the hook, helping the listener feel less anxious about the situation. The speaker, however, is still left with the issue to deal with. This can make the speaker feel hopeless, helpless, or angry. The negative emotion in the listener—anxiety—is thus transferred to the speaker, who has to cope with the original situation along with the new emotions raised by the listener's denial.

As listeners, we seldom want to admit that we don't care enough to listen. Denial strategies can help us feel like we have listened appropriately. Isn't good listening evidenced by the fact that we're saying something related in some way to the person's problem? Denial also reflects a simplistic view of the world: all problems actually have easy solutions, and we just need to find those straightforward answers. Humility helps us live in a world where answers don't always come easily.

Interrogating

Sandra might approach Mary with a series of questions, hoping the questions would help Mary think through her options. "What solutions have you tried? What do you think is the cause of the anxiety inside you? Why do you think you feel so strongly about this? Have you talked with any friends about why this is bothering you so much?" Too many questions can have the opposite effect of what was intended. The barrage of questions can make the speaker feel defensive, exposed, and distracted from the main issue.

A rapid-fire series of questions can come from the drive to action. Let's solve this now! Interrogating can also come from all the same anxieties described in the previous paragraphs, which raise adrenaline and can make people talk quickly. To ask questions one at a time and listen carefully to the answer requires patience and self-control. Humility in the listener can empower and enable some of that patience and self-control, as the listener acknowledges inwardly that the best solution must necessarily come from the person with the problem, not from outside. [3]

Offering solutions, judging, denying, and interrogating are easy to do. They help lower our anxiety as listeners, because we believe we're doing something in response to the words we hear, and doing something—anything—helps us feel more in control and more competent. In my experience, the challenge of avoiding these four ineffective listening strategies never ends. I've been trying to grow in competence as a listener for most of my adult life, and I've been studying listening intensely for the past five years. However, I still tend to jump to possible solutions, judgments, easy answers, and aggressive questions, particularly when I'm feeling an uncomfortable emotion in a conversation or when I'm tired and running out of listening energy.

At the same time that I emphasize that these strategies help the listener rather than the speaker by transferring the listener's own anxiety to the other person, I also affirm that some aspects of these strategies can be helpful at the right time. Sometimes brainstorming solutions is helpful, sometimes the speaker benefits from hearing encouragement that the problem can be solved, and sometimes asking questions can be exactly the right thing to do. The challenge in avoiding the roadblocks described above lies in the willingness of the listener to engage gently with the speaker's issue, rather than blocking listening in order to feel more comfortable him or herself.

HUMILITY AND HONESTY

The strategies for coping with anxiety, described at the end of the previous chapter, depend on humility. To acknowledge that I'm feeling a mix of emotions but choosing to park those emotions to the side and concentrate on listening to the person in front of me puts his needs ahead of my own. We manifest the meekness and submission that are characteristics of humility when we give priority to the needs of others in conversations.

Jumping in with a packet of advice indicates that I believe I have answers to problems, while setting aside my love of problem solving in a conversation demonstrates that I know I am not responsible for all the problems I hear. God knows the answers, and yes, sometimes I'm called to participate in those answers. But when I'm in a conversation, my first responsibility is to focus on the needs of the other person. Humility is required to be willing to shift the focus from myself to others and to acknowledge that I am not the source of all wisdom in solving a problem.

My spiritual director believes humility is closely related to honesty. Both false humility and excessive pride, she believes, display a lack of honesty about ourselves or about the situation. Affirming some simple truths can help us rest in the kind of humility that nurtures good listening. Those truths include:

- I am not responsible for solving every problem for others.
- I am not always the best source of advice.
- I am not the only person with things on his or her mind, or issues to face, or a busy schedule.

Perhaps the biggest truth I need to remember as a listener is that I am not the center of the universe. Because that's true, I can set aside the intense emotions I might be feeling in a conversation.

I am deeply concerned that people of faith are exhorted over and over to care for others, but the listening skills that might demonstrate some of that care, and might help us understand how to care, are not taught. The skills described in chapter 8 are quite easy to teach, and yet we ignore them. The anxiety issues described in chapter 9 and the lack of humility in listening described in this chapter inhibit a great deal of listening, yet in congregations we so seldom acknowledge them, and we don't give people tools to cope with them. I long for congregational leaders to validate the significance of listening skills as an essential part of caring relationships and as a necessary tool for mission and evangelism. The "slow food" movement has been gaining attention in recent years as a way to eat more healthily and rediscover the joy of food and eating. I would love to see a "slow listening" movement in congregations to build relationships and rediscover the joy of true curiosity about what others are thinking and feeling.

QUESTIONS FOR REFLECTION, JOURNALING, AND GROUP DISCUSSION

- When you hear the word "humility," what are your reactions? In what ways do you think you manifest humility that avoids the two pitfalls of excessive humility or pride? In what settings do you tend to fall into one of the two pitfalls related to humility? In your own life, what are the connections between humility and honesty?
- Think about a listener you know whom you think shows healthy humility in conversations. Which listening skills does that person use most often? What do you observe about the way he or she uses those skills?
- In what settings or with what people are you most likely to launch into solution giving and problem solving? What do you think triggers that response? What might help you reduce your tendency to jump into problem solving in conversations?
- Four roadblocks to listening are described in this chapter: solution giving, judging, denying, and interrogating. Which one of these do you find yourself using most often? What are some of the reasons why you find that strategy comfortable? Have you seen negative repercussions from using those roadblocks?
- What goals related to humility and honesty might you adopt for yourself as a listener? Write a prayer for yourself as a listener, focusing on those goals. Write a prayer for your congregation about growing in humility and honesty in listening.
- Think of someone you know who seems to be an appropriately humble listener (no false or pretend humility!). Pay that person a compliment for the ability to meld humility and listening, and ask what influences motivated him or her to embrace humility.

11

LISTENING, RECEPTIVITY, AND SPEAKING UP

There is a difference between understanding and agreeing with a speaker. We need to develop new psychological habits that encourage us to keep an open mind and a positive attitude to the motivation behind what is communicated to us orally.

—Terry Mohan, Helen McGregor, Shirley Saunders, and Ray Archee, *Communicating! Theory and Practice*[1]

As I mentioned in the preface, I interviewed sixty-three ministers and lay leaders about the significance of listening in congregational life. When I described my research at the beginning of each interview, I explained my conviction that in order to engage more effectively in mission and ministry, congregational leaders need to teach listening skills and nurture an environment that affirms listening. Sixty-two of my interviewees agreed with my conviction. Anita was the one interviewee who disagreed, and her words illuminate one more listening challenge. When is it appropriate to speak up? When does listening become a defensive posture that impedes speaking honestly and forthrightly about what we believe?

Anita works in publishing, and she lives in an English village on the outskirts of a small city. She and her husband attend the local Anglican parish church, which meets in a nine-hundred-year-old church building. Anita described the congregation as very traditional and well supported by the community. The congregation, she said, has many "village-like" activities," including numerous committees, and members have a strong ethos of pastoral care for one another. "People come to our church because we do love each other. 'See how they love one another' could be our theme verse. A lot of people feel the warm fuzzy but don't know what it means." Anita and her husband desire to encourage deeper commitment to Christ within their congregation, and in response to that desire they have led numerous Emmaus courses. The Emmaus course is designed to bring people to faith in Christ and to encourage discipleship among people who are already Christians.[2]

After hearing about my research, Anita expressed a counter-premise:

> In our church we have been paralyzed by listening and have ignored the mandate to share the Gospel. We listen to the culture, to climate change, to the Muslims and Hindus around us. There's so much cultural noise, and we listen to all of it. We also listen well on Sunday mornings. We have two full minutes of silence after the sermon. Three or four times a year we have a quiet day retreat from ten to four. Silence and hearing God speak are valued in this congregation. However, listening has caused us to lose the power of speech. We want to be conciliatory. We don't want to offend. Everyone's listening really hard but no one is proclaiming anything. Listening hasn't produced the fruit of reaching out.

Anita draws a distinction between a congregation that ministers to the people within and a congregation that is willing to get beyond itself. When members of a congregation are willing to engage beyond their doors, Anita believes there's a willingness to say, "Here's my path; tell me about yours." This results in an honest give and take where both parties can speak honestly about what they believe. Anita has observed that in her congregation, the approach to people both inside or outside the congregation with differing viewpoints is: "'Yes, I hear you, I value you as a person, I'm affirming you by listening to you, I love you, I'll back off.' We equate listening with acceptance." She also believes that in her congregation, "We spend too much time on the sensitive inner journey and too little time on the demands of the Gospel, so we miss opportunities."

Anita's comments illustrate the dangers of equating listening with acceptance. Her comments also affirm the way that a listening stance can become so comfortable that we stop speaking up about what matters to us and what we believe. In addition, she's right that listening can become a defense against conflict. We fear that if we let others know what we really think or believe, they will disagree in an unpleasant way, and we will feel uncomfortable. "Yes, I hear you, I love you, and I'll back off" defends us against unpleasantness so we feel comfortable.

A good number of my interviewees talked about the discomfort many Christians feel when the topic of God or issues of faith come up in conversations with people who don't attend church. Rachel, the vicar of an Anglican church in England, has observed that people often feel anxious in conversations with those outside the church because they have preconceived negative ideas about what evangelism is. Many Christians have absorbed the message that they need to tell people about the Gospel, but they don't know how. Rachel believes Christians need to have confidence in their own faith story and they need to develop the right vocabulary in order to converse with people outside the church about questions of faith. Rachel said she aims to help the members of her congregation gain confidence in sharing their own faith story, and in proclaiming "in simple words" what they believe to be true about God. This takes time, she has observed.

She went on to talk about what evangelism is. Most people, she asserted, believe evangelism consists solely of proclamation. While simple and clear proclamation is a skill that she hopes everyone will learn, she also emphasized the ability to ask good questions about people's hopes and concerns, their values and priorities. She longs to see Christians become confident asking the "God questions," the kinds of questions that help people to open up about their own spiritual searching, questions, and beliefs. In addition, she longs for people to learn the listening skills that would help them hear and receive others' opinions and views without feeling threatened. Too often, Rachel said, Christians are afraid they won't know what to say in response to people's comments and questions about God. They are also anxious that they might have to move into more of a proclamation mode, which would feel uncomfortable, so in conversations they simply don't engage with topics related to God.

I'm sure Anita would agree with Rachel that many, if not most, Christians lack the ability to state simply and clearly what they believe, and they also lack the confidence to do that in diverse settings. However, the context for making those statements needs to be a back-and-forth conversation focused on spiritual issues and life priorities. Asking good questions, a key listening skill, helps make those conversations happen. Another key listening skill is the ability to cope with the anxiety that arises within us when we hear how utterly different another person's viewpoint is from our own. And the humility that characterizes good listening and enables us to listen carefully and speak our own truth gently is one more essential listening skill related to proclamation of the Gospel. There can be no effective proclamation without commensurate listening. Three terms I mentioned in the first chapter—holy curiosity, holy listening, and receptivity—help illuminate this question of speaking up appropriately, raised by Anita's comments.

HOLY CURIOSITY

Curiosity can take two forms. One version of curiosity is nosy and prying, and it comes across as invasive. That kind of curiosity arises out of the listener's need to know all the details about a person's situation, perhaps so the listener can gossip with others about it or appear to be knowledgeable in other settings. A more subtle form of invasive curiosity arises when we feel proud of our listening abilities, so we draw people out in order to demonstrate our listening skills, so we can feel good about ourselves. Any self-focused listening can slide into being nosy and prying. That's why minimal encouragers and reflection are such important listening tools. They allow our conversation partners to change the subject when they're ready to do so. A constant stream of questions on the part of listeners does not give speakers the freedom to stop talking about a topic when they feel they have said enough.

In contrast to nosy and invasive curiosity, the second form involves being interested and concerned, eager to understand the other person's interests, priorities, and experiences if she wants to talk about them. When the listener is motivated by God's love, then this form of curiosity becomes holy curiosity, which undergirds the kinds of conversations in congregations, workplaces, and homes where people are able to express the overlap of their faith and their daily lives. Holy curiosity makes possible pastoral care listening and listening for mission, and it lays a foundation for proclamation of the Christian Gospel.

Anita talked about the fact that the people in her congregation listen to what the media says about culture, values, and other religions, and she's right that what Christians hear from the media is often intimidating. "Society is becoming more secular at an increasing rate," the news commentator intones, and those comments create unease and even fear among people of faith. "The increasing presence of people of other religions— Muslims, Hindus, and Buddhists—is changing the face of our cities and towns, and new tolerance is needed," a newspaper article reports, and members of congregations wonder what the implications will be for them. News items about politics and religion, science and religion, and medical ethics and religion raise complex issues. So much information related to religion that is conveyed by the media raises anxiety.

While listening to the wider culture is a good idea in order to keep pace with the signs of the times, our most important listening focuses on individuals. It's a good idea to read an online article about what Hindus believe so I can understand the background my new Hindu neighbors bring with them, but how much better to talk with my new neighbors using holy curiosity to ask about their lives and priorities. Listening to a news report about patterns of income inequality to understand the issue is a good idea, but how much better to have a conversation—seasoned with holy curiosity—with the person at work who is paid much less or much more than I am, with the goal of trying to understand that person's concerns and values. The priority Jesus put on listening to individuals is instructive. Jesus proclaimed the Gospel in a context of deep and careful listening to specific men and women with ordinary needs and concerns. I believe part of the problem in Anita's congregation comes from too much listening to the media about people with diverse viewpoints and too little holy curiosity in conversations with individuals.

Obstacles to holy curiosity come in several forms. The quotation at the beginning of this chapter notes the difference between understanding what a speaker is saying and agreeing with it. This key distinction plays a significant role in holy curiosity. So much of the fear that impedes listening in everyday settings comes from not truly believing that we can grow in understanding the priorities and values that lie behind another person's convictions without agreeing with them. Listening often changes us because we understand more about how other people think and feel, but listening does not necessarily mean that we change our own central beliefs in response. Holy curiosity enables us to try to understand others' beliefs and priorities, being open to change within ourselves but also being open to holding strongly to our own convictions.

Another obstacle to holy curiosity is the conviction that we already know what the other person means when they say something. One of my friends read over the chapter where I described my upsetting stay in the hospital, and afterward she asked me to talk about that time. I mentioned one nurse who was like an anchor to me while I was there. At that point my friend commented that she was glad the nurse was helpful to me. Later in the conversation my friend returned to the topic, saying she hadn't asked more about why the nurse meant so much to me simply because she assumed she already knew what made a nurse helpful. It took her until later in the conversation for her holy curiosity to come into play, making her wonder what I had particularly appreciated about that nurse.

Holy curiosity is a lovely thing, but we don't have to use it 24/7. During the past year, when friends and colleagues have asked me what I'm doing these days, I have usually told them I'm writing a book on listening. In response, numerous people have asked me if we are obligated to keep listening to people who talk too much, who circle around the same topic over and over, or who jump from one topic to the next without seeming to take a breath. I have assured all of them that sometimes it is perfectly appropriate to stop listening. Listening is not an end in itself, a tool that should be used continually and endlessly. Sometimes, when conversing with someone who is talking a lot, the only way to stop the flow of words is to change the subject or even walk away from the conversation with a quick word of farewell. Sometimes, however, holy curiosity can come into play in guiding those kinds of frustrating conversations. Rather than being disgusted that my conversation partner can't seem to stop talking, I can try to summon up curiosity about why the topic is so significant in that person's life. I might try to move the conversation to a deeper level, saying something like, "This seems like such a big topic for you right now. I find myself wondering why it's so significant to you." Or perhaps, "I can hear a lot of energy about that incident. I wonder if you can see any overlaps between that incident and your beliefs about God." Holy curiosity helps us wonder about "the need that lies behind the need," as one of my interviewees phrased it.

HOLY LISTENING

In chapter 1 I referred to the term "holy listening," which Craig Satterlee uses to describe listening that seeks to discern "the presence and activity of God in the joys, struggles, and hopes of the ordinary activities of congregational life, as well as the uncertainty and opportunity of change and transition."[3] I see holy curiosity as one aspect of the larger skill of holy listening, and I see holy listening as relevant to activities within a congregation, as Satterlee indicates, but also applicable to conversations in every setting in life.

What makes listening holy? The word "holy" means set apart, consecrated to God or to a religious purpose. The kind of listening I have been advocating throughout this book has several purposes, all of which seem to me to be holy:

- understanding the viewpoints of others in order to serve them, respect them, pray for them, or respond appropriately and lovingly to what they have said
- allowing people to talk through the events and concerns of their life, so they can articulate the way their faith has intersected with those events and concerns
- paying attention to God's voice in order to draw near in love and obedience, for individuals and for groups

In Anita's church, listening has fueled fear and the inability to speak up. That kind of listening cannot be considered holy.

Issues of appropriate communication in evangelism illustrate some of the key issues of speaking up versus listening, even though evangelism is, of course, only one kind of conversation that is "set apart, consecrated to God or to a religious purpose." I wish that Anita's congregational leaders could talk with the leaders of one of the Presbyterian congregations in my city. This congregation has been teaching evangelism skills using the language of "three stories" to help people understand how to talk comfortably about their faith with anyone.[4] The leaders of this congregation argue that evangelism always begins with the story of the person who is not a Christian. The Christian's first step is being in a relationship with people and paying attention to their lives. This involves noticing unspoken communication such as dress, body language, an item of jewelry, or something they have done. The purpose of the noticing is to elicit stories about the events, values, and priorities that have shaped that person by asking "wondering" questions. Obviously, drawing out those stories requires listening carefully, particularly reflecting along the lines of, "So what I thought I heard you say was . . ." The second step in evangelism, as taught in this particular church, is telling our own stories about what has shaped us and where God fits in our story. This step may happen in the first conversation or, more likely, it may take much longer to get there. The third step is recounting God's story.

This "three stories" approach to evangelism requires listening skills for the first step, and confidence and clarity for the second and third steps. Listening remains essential, but speaking up also matters. The congregational leaders who teach this process emphasize that people should practice telling their own story and God's story until they can do so clearly and briefly. The situation in Anita's congregation has set up a false dichotomy between listening and speaking up, and the "three stories" version of evangelism illustrates the potential close relationship of the two. In the Gospels, Jesus listens well but also speaks uncompromisingly and with great relevance to each person he talks to. We simply cannot speak with pertinence unless we listen, and holy listening often leads us to say something in response. But we also cannot use listening as a defense against speaking.

My husband, Dave, recently said his priority in evangelism is "paying attention, reflecting back, and then paying attention again to try to notice what a person's words reflect about the person and their values. This helps us figure out what we can discuss as fellow travelers." He agrees that listening and talking both play a role in evangelism, and in fact in almost every relationship. He went on to say that "holy listening implies keeping one ear cocked to what God might be saying. Maybe you could call it 'augmented listening.'" Holy listening in his view, then, is a form of double listening, and Dave believes holy or "augmented" listening plays a role in many different kinds of conversations, including evangelism.

The term "double listening" has been used in this book to refer to many aspects of listening for mission and ministry. Celia, a Baptist pastor and spiritual director, is another person who advocates trying to listen to God while listening to others. This helps her stay open to what God might be saying to her while she listens: "I learn so much when I listen to others. It's like doorways opening." She reflected that in conversations, we need "a kind of appreciative inquiry,"[5] which she describes as interest and acceptance instead of judgment, asking how people understand an issue, which enriches everyone.

Celia went on to discuss the way listening helps people get in touch with what they themselves believe, another form of holy listening that involves paying attention to multiple layers of meaning. She reflected,

> Listening often helps people become conscious of what they're saying. It helps them make connections they haven't seen before. People say, "I've never said that before. I wonder if that's right." We can journal or talk to ourselves, and things come up. Why is it so different, so much richer, when we talk to others and they listen?

The richness that Celia has observed in conversations comes at least in part from the many listening skills discussed in this book. When I have taught listening skills to my students, they have expressed surprise at two things: first, that listening skills are actually fairly simple to describe, and second, that it's so easy to fall into a rut of using certain listening skills but not others. Many students have said that some straightforward instruction on listening skills made a quantum difference in their ability to listen, because they gained confidence in using a variety of listening skills. In our congregations, growing in confidence in listening will help people engage in the kind of conversations Celia describes, as well as the "three story" evangelism advocated by the Presbyterian congregation in my city. Listening skills facilitate holy listening and speaking up when the time is right.

RECEPTIVITY

Another term that helps summarize many of the themes in this book is "receptivity," my latest favorite word. In the past couple of years, I've been trying to grow in being more receptive to what God is doing all around me. I've been trying to notice the gifts God is offering me through my work, my home, my body, and the people in my life. I've been trying to control my life less and instead receive the gifts of my life with open hands. A key component of a receptive life is listening to God and to others, thus the concept of receptivity summarizes many of the themes of this book.

When two people have an honest discussion about where God seems present in daily life, those individuals are trying to be receptive to each other's perceptions as well as to God. When someone has a conversation with a workmate who holds totally different political convictions, with the goal of trying to understand how he arrived at those convictions, the listener is trying to be receptive to another person's reality. When members of a congregation listen to the wider community in order to try to figure out where they can make a difference, they are trying to be receptive to the actual needs and concerns in the community.

Around the year 2000 I read *Making Room: Recovering Hospitality as a Christian Tradition* by Christine Pohl,[6] which immediately joined the short list of books that have changed my life. Pohl nudged me to see not just the significance of acts of hospitality involving food and lodging, but also to see hospitality as a paradigm for all relationships and all ministry. I began to try to be hospitable in every interaction with people. I'm sure this shift toward being hospitable played a role in my growing interest in listening skills. And I know my commitment to trying to be hospitable in every conversation brought into focus this posture of receptivity that has been so significant in my life in recent years.

Sitting around a table eating a meal together breaks down barriers. When I'm eating with someone who has political views that are different from mine and that person starts talking about those views, I try to listen. In fact, I have to listen, at least to some extent, because I can't get up and walk away like I can in so many other settings. One of my interviewees talked about shared hospitality promoting a "different kind of listening." When I eat with people, I am somehow more open to hearing their viewpoint. Food breaks down barriers and often brings a kind of magic to conversations. Pohl's book encouraged me to bring that attitude, that magic, into all of life. Of course I don't always succeed, but I'm trying to be more receptive to whatever people bring into a conversation. I'm trying to be hospitable in all settings, and listening skills are essential to that stance.

In our time, practicing that attitude of hospitality and receptivity requires us to make some careful and intentional choices. Slowing down in the midst of a busy schedule, so hard to achieve, is usually required. Multitasking, which divides our attention, must be set aside for a period of time. Also necessary is ignoring the ringtone of the cell phone, the music on the iPod, or the lure of the Internet at our fingertips on the smart phone. One of my interviewees pointed out that technology points us to the next thing, which takes us out of the present and turns our focus onto ourselves and nurtures narcissism. An attitude of receptivity requires abandoning that future focus and narcissism in order to be present to this moment and this person.

Receptivity includes being open to God's guidance, and in any conversation, God may guide me to speak up about something. Receptivity does not mean being silent all the time. Some of us need encouragement to speak up more often, and some of us need encouragement to listen more, and in every conversation all of us need God's guidance regarding both listening and speaking. A willingness to be receptive to God's nudging about speaking and listening might help the people in Anita's congregation let go of some of their fear about speaking up about what they believe.

Listening is not an end in itself. Listening skills are tools that put us in a receptive, hospitable posture so we can appreciate, learn from, encourage, and speak wisely to the people in our lives. Listening skills help us learn how and where to serve individuals and local communities. Listening skills facilitate the kinds of conversations where we can talk about the overlap of our faith and our daily lives, and the ability to talk about and recognize that intersection shapes us into people who can participate in mission and ministry with energy, enthusiasm, wisdom, and love. In a follow-up email, one of my interviewees wrote, "Many of us may not choose to share information about ourselves unless asked by someone we know to be a good and interested listener." I long for our congregations to be places where good and interested listeners are nurtured.

QUESTIONS FOR REFLECTION, JOURNALING, AND GROUP DISCUSSION

- How would you respond to Anita's comments at the beginning of this chapter? In what settings have you seen listening impede speaking up? In what settings have you seen listening become a defensive posture?
- Spend some time pondering the terms "holy curiosity" and "holy listening." In what settings have you seen curiosity become invasive and nosy? In your opinion, what makes curiosity holy? What makes listening holy? In what ways can holy curiosity and holy listening help people know when to listen and when to speak up?
- What would you like to be more receptive to? What do you think your congregation needs to be more receptive to? What steps would be

necessary, both in your life and in your congregation, to make that receptivity a reality?

- Write a prayer for yourself as a listener. Consider using "holy curiosity," "holy listening," or "receptivity" in your prayer. Use the prayer to sum up what you have learned from this book.

- Think about the person who has listened to you the most consistently over your life. Pay that person a compliment, express your thanks, and say what difference his or her listening has made to you.

NOTES

PREFACE

1. Dietrich Bonhoeffer, *Life Together* (London: SCM, 1967), 75.
2. www.stephenministries.org.
3. Eugene Peterson, *Answering God: Learning to Pray from the Psalms* (London: Marshall Pickering, 1989), 1.

1. A CALL TO LISTEN

1. www.uk.alpha.org, www.alphausa.org.
2. Robert Bolton, "Listening Is More Than Merely Hearing," in John Steward, ed., *Bridges Not Walls: A Book about Interpersonal Communication* (New York: McGraw-Hill, 1990), 177.
3. "Holy and Active Listening" by Craig Satterlee, downloaded June 21, 2012, from http://www.alban.org/conversation.aspx?id=2146&terms=listening. Adapted from *When God Speaks through Change: Preaching in Times of Congregational Transformation* (Bethesda, MD: The Alban Institute, 2005).
4. Ibid.
5. "Education: Holy Curiosity," *Time Magazine* 53, no. 12 (March 21, 1949): 49.
6. Winn Collier, *Holy Curiosity: Encountering Jesus' Provocative Questions* (Grand Rapids, MI: Baker Books, 2008).
7. Amy Hollingsworth, *Holy Curiosity: Cultivating the Creative Spirit in Everyday Life* (Eugene, OR: Cascade Books, 2011).

2. LISTENING TO THE UNSPOKEN

1. Robert Bolton, "Listening Is More Than Merely Hearing," in John Stewart, ed., *Bridges Not Walls: A Book about Interpersonal Communication* (New York: McGraw-Hill, 1990), 175.

2. "Perhaps the most clear statement on the record from Barth concerning these matters comes from a *Time Magazine* piece on Barth published on Friday, May 31, 1963. '[Barth] recalls that 40 years ago he advised young theologians "to take your Bible and take your newspaper, and read both. But interpret newspapers from your Bible."'" Downloaded on March 27, 2013 from the website http://wiki.answers.com/Q/Did_Karl_Barth_say_you_must_hold_the_Bible _in_one_hand _and_the_newspaper_in_the_other.

3. John R. W. Stott, *The Contemporary Christian: An Urgent Plea for Double Listening* (Downer's Grove, IL: InterVarsity Press, 1992), 27–28.

4. Paul Windsor, "And Chairs," *Unpacking* Blog. Downloaded April 1, 2013 from http://paulwindsor.blogspot.co.nz/2006/05/and-chairs.html.

5. Stott, *The Contemporary Christian: An Urgent Plea for Double Listening*, 27–28.

6. Brian Walsh and Richard Middleton, *The Transforming Vision: Shaping a Christian Worldview* (Downer's Grove, IL: IVP Academic, 2005).

7. Howard A. Snyder, *Earthcurrents* (Nashville: Abingdon, 1995).

8. Heather McCracken, "Under 30s loneliest of all age groups, survey finds," *Otago Daily Times*, April 24, 2013, 3.

3. LISTENING WITHIN THE CONGREGATION

1. Richard Dimbelby and Graeme Burton, *More Than Words: An Introduction to Communication*, 4th ed. (London: Routledge, 2007), 88.

2. Nancy Tatom Ammerman describes her research in *Sacred Stories, Spiritual Tribes: Finding Religion in Everyday Life* (New York: Oxford University Press, 2013). I heard her talk about her research before the release of the book in her two keynote addresses on June 29 and July 1, 2013, at the Australia New Zealand Association for Theological Schools annual conference, held at Laidlaw College in Auckland. All of the descriptions of her research in this section come from her two keynote addresses that I heard.

4. LISTENING FOR MISSION

1. Robert Bolton, "Listening Is More Than Merely Hearing," in John Stewart, ed., *Bridges Not Walls: A Book about Interpersonal Communication* (New York: McGraw-Hill, 1990), 183–84.

5. LISTENING IN CONSENSUS AND DISCERNMENT

1. Martin B. Copenhaver, "Decide or Discern," *The Christian Century*, December 28, 2010.

2. The latest revision of *Getting to Yes: Negotiating Agreement Without Giving In* has three authors: Roger Fisher, William L. Ury, and Bruce Patton (New York: Penguin Books, 2011).

3. Tim Challies, "Defining Discernment." Downloaded June 12, 2013 from http://www.challies.com/discernment/defining-discernment-0.

4. John MacArthur, "What Is Discernment and Why Is It Important?" Downloaded June 12, 2013 from http://www.gty.org/Resources/Questions/QA138.

5. Jon Krakauer, *Under the Banner of Heaven: A Story of Violent Faith* (Flushing, MI: Anchor Group, 2004).

6. LISTENING TO GOD TOGETHER THROUGH SCRIPTURE

1. Paul Byer developed the manuscript method of inductive Bible study in the early 1950s as a staff worker with InterVarsity Christian Fellowship. I experienced his leadership of Bible study retreats using the manuscript method many times in the 1970s and 1980s, and I am deeply indebted to him for enabling me to hear God's voice through the scriptures so vividly and for modeling a powerful and participatory style of Bible study.

2. Bill Bishop, *The Big Sort: Why the Clustering of Like-Minded America Is Tearing us Apart* (Boston: Mariner Books, 2009).

3. My book *Joy Together: Spiritual Practices for Your Congregation* (Louisville, KY: Westminster John Knox Press, 2012) has an entire chapter on communal contemplative approaches to the Bible, with many more examples for leading *lectio divina* in groups than I can offer here.

4. Gabriel O'Donnell, "Reading for Holiness: *Lectio Divina*," in Robin Maas and Gabriel O'Donnell, O.P., eds., *Spiritual Traditions for the Contemporary Church* (Nashville: Abingdon, 1990), 47.

7. LISTENING TO GOD TOGETHER THROUGH SPIRITUAL PRACTICES

1. M. Robert Mulholland Jr., "Prayer as Availability to God," *Weavings* 12, no. 5 (September/October 1997): 26.

2. Richard Foster, *A Celebration of Discipline* (San Francisco: Harper & Row, 1978, 1988).

3. Marjorie Thompson, *Soul Feast: An Invitation to the Christian Spiritual Life* (Louisville, KY: Westminster John Knox Press, 1995, 2005), xv.

4. Adele Ahlberg Calhoun, *Spiritual Disciplines Handbook* (Downers Grove, IL: InterVarsity Press, 2005), 17.

5. Lynne M. Baab, *Fasting: Spiritual Freedom Beyond Our Appetites* (Downer's Grove, IL: InterVarsity Press, 2006), 124–26.

6. Lynne M. Baab, *Joy Together: Spiritual Practices for Your Congregation* (Louisville, KY: Westminster John Knox Press, 2012), 54.

7. This story is described in greater detail in my book *Joy Together: Spiritual Practices for Your Congregation*, 151–52.

8. David Hansen, *Long Wandering Prayer* (Downer's Grove, IL: InterVarsity Press, 2001).

9. M. Robert Mulholland Jr., "Prayer as Availability to God," 20–26.

10. Ibid., 26.

11. In 2006, a twentieth-anniversary edition of *Open Mind, Open Heart* by Thomas Keating was published by Continuum (New York), with updated language, a new preface, and an expanded glossary.

8. THE LISTENING TOOLBOX

1. Voncile Smith, "Listening," in Owen Hargie, ed., *A Handbook of Communication Skills* (London: Croom Helm, 1986), 251.

2. The forms of nonverbal communication listed in this paragraph and the previous paragraph come from Richard Dimbelby and Graeme Burton, *More Than Words: An Introduction to Communication*, 4th ed. (London: Routledge, 2007), 44–49.

3. This list of minimal encouragers comes from Robert Bolton, "Listening Is More Than Merely Hearing," in John Stewart, ed., *Bridges Not Walls: A Book about Interpersonal Communication* (New York: McGraw-Hill, 1990), 186.

4. Ibid., 188.

5. The first two sentences in this paragraph and the benefits of silence in the previous paragraph come from Bolton, "Listening Is More Than Merely Hearing," 189.

6. The material about questions is adapted from Rosalie Maggio, *The Art of Talking to Anyone* (New York: McGraw-Hill, 2005), 45–53.

7. The material on appropriate and inappropriate uses of reflecting is adapted from Robert J. Martin, *A Skills and Strategies Handbook for Working with People* (Eaglewood Cliffs, NJ: 1983), 45–46.

8. Kathleen S. Verderber and Rudolph F. Verderber, *Inter-Act: Interpersonal Communication Concepts, Skills and Contexts*, 10th ed. (New York: Oxford University Press, 2004), 211.

9. Ibid., 214.

10. Jamil Zaki, "What, Me Care? Young Are Less Empathetic," *Scientific American*, January 19, 2011, downloaded January 5, 2013 from http://www.scientificamerican.com/article.cfm?id=what-me-care.

11. The list of empathy blockers and a few of the examples come from Terry Mohan, Helen McGregor, Shirley Saunders, and Ray Archee, *Communicating! Theory and Practice*, 4th ed. (Sydney: Harcourt Brace, 1992), 409. Most of the examples are mine.

12. The four contrasts described in this section come from Joseph DeVito, Susan O'Rourke, and Linda O'Neill, *Human Communication: New Zealand Edition* (Auckland: Pearson Education, 2000), 68–72. The comments about each contrast are my own.

9. ANXIETY AND LISTENING

1. Robert Bolton, "Listening Is More Than Merely Hearing," in John Stewart, ed., *Bridges Not Walls: A Book about Interpersonal Communication* (New York: McGraw-Hill, 1990), 189.

2. Terry Mohan, Helen McGregor, Shirley Saunders, and Ray Archee, *Communicating! Theory and Practice*, 4th ed. (Sydney: Harcourt Brace, 1992), 418.

3. The Four Spiritual Laws were written in the 1950s by Bill Bright, the founder of Campus Crusade, an evangelical Christian student movement. The four spiritual laws are:

- God loves you and offers a wonderful plan for your life (John 3:16, John 10:10).
- Man is sinful and separated from God. Therefore, he cannot know and experience God's love and plan for his life (Romans 3:23, Romans 6:23).

- Jesus Christ is God's only provision for man's sin. Through Him you can know and experience God's love and plan for your life (Romans 5:8, I Corinthians 15:3–6, John 14:6).
- We must individually receive Jesus Christ as Savior and Lord; then we can know and experience God's love and plan for our lives (John 1:12, Ephesians 2:8,9, John 3:1–8, Revelation 3:20).

Downloaded on January 19, 2013, from the site http://campuscrusade.com/four-lawseng.htm.

4. I am grateful to Jayme Koerselman for the idea of parking anxiety somewhere while we are talking. Jayme teaches counseling at Laidlaw College in Auckland, New Zealand.

5. Some popular books about the Enneagram include: *The Wisdom of the Enneagram* by Don Richard Riso and Russ Hudson (New York: Bantam, 1999), *The Enneagram: Understanding Yourself and the Others in Your Life* by Helen Palmer (New York: HarperOne, 1991), and *The Enneagram: A Christian Perspective* by Richard Rohr and Andreas Ebert (New York: Crossroads Publishing Company, 2001).

10. HUMILITY AND LISTENING

1. Terry Mohan, Helen McGregor, Shirley Saunders, and Ray Archee, *Communicating! Theory and Practice*, 4th ed. (Sydney: Harcourt Brace, 1992), 404.

2. Philip Yancey, *What's So Amazing About Grace?* (Grand Rapids: Zondervan Publishing House, 1997), 70.

3. The four roadblocks to listening were described by Richard Bolstad and Margot Hamblett in *Transforming Communication* (Auckland: Longman, 1997), 88–89.

11. LISTENING, RECEPTIVITY, AND SPEAKING UP

1. Terry Mohan, Helen McGregor, Shirley Saunders, and Ray Archee, *Communicating! Theory and Practice*, 4th ed. (Sydney: Harcourt Brace, 1992), 417.

2. http://www.chpublishing.co.uk/emmaus.

3. "Holy and Active Listening" by Craig Satterlee, downloaded June 21, 2012, from http://www.alban.org/conversation.aspx?id=2146 &terms=listening. Adapted from *When God Speaks through Change: Preaching in Times of Congregational Transformation* (Bethesda, MD: The Alban Institute, 2005).

4. The leaders of this congregation told me they got their idea from *God Space: Where Spiritual Conversations Happen Naturally* by Doug Pollock (Loveland, CO: Group Publishing, 2009).

5. The process of appreciative inquiry involves listening within an organization (or congregation), in response to questions about the congregation's strengths. Case Western Reserve University's Weatherhead School of Management has set up a website devoted to sharing resources and tools related to appreciative inquiry: http://appreciativeinquiry.case.edu/. One of the books in the Appendix describes what that process looks like in a congregation.

6. Christine Pohl, *Making Room: Rediscovering Hospitality as a Christian Tradition* (Grand Rapids, MI: Eerdmans, 1999).

FOR FURTHER READING

BOOKS ON LISTENING

Hedahl, Susan K. *Listening Ministry: Rethinking Pastoral Leadership* (Minneapolis: Fortress, 2001). Hedahl argues that effective listening undergirds all ministry, and she presents biblical, historical, and theological background for the significance of listening in pastoral and worship settings.

Lindahl, Kay. *The Sacred Art of Listening: Forty Reflections for Cultivating a Spiritual Practice* (Woodstock, VT: Skylight Paths, 2003). Lindahl encourages slowing down, becoming comfortable with silence and being present with others deeply. Lindahl also wrote a companion guide: *Practicing the Sacred Art of Listening: A Guide to Enrich Your Relationships and Kindle Your Spiritual Life* (Woodstock, VT: Skylight Paths, 2003).

Long, Anne. *Listening* (London: Darton, Longman and Todd, 1990). Long emphasizes the role of listening in bringing emotional healing to the person being listened to. A powerful book about listening in pastoral care and healing prayer.

Pembroke, Neil. *The Art of Listening: Dialogue, Shame and Pastoral Care* (London: T & T Clark, 2002). Pembroke draws on psychoanalytic approaches to listening and shows their relevance in pastoral care and counseling.

Savage, John. *Listening and Caring Skills: A Guide for Groups and Leaders* (Nashville: Abingdon Press, 2010). A clear presentation of listening skills with helpful information on how to look behind the words we hear to the conversation partner's emotions and priorities.

BOOKS ON DISCERNMENT AND LISTENING TO GOD

Ackerman, John. *Listening to God: Spiritual Formation in Congregations* (Herndon, VA: The Alban Institute, 2001). Ackerman advocates listening to God communally as the foundation for congregational growth in faith and awareness of God's presence in individuals and in the community.

Barton, Ruth Haley. *Pursuing God's Will Together: A Discernment Practice for Leadership Groups* (Downer's Grove, IL: IVP Books, 2012). Barton advocates communal discernment on the part of church leaders and lays out steps in the discernment process.

Fendall, Lon, Jan Wood, and Bruce Bishop. *Practicing Discernment Together: Finding God's Way Forward in Decision Making* (Newberg, OR: Barclay Press, 2007). The authors draw on the Quaker tradition to discuss communal discernment, offering examples, practical suggestions, and three extended case studies.

Friesen, Garry. *Decision Making and the Will of God* (Colorado Springs, CO: Multnomah Books, 2004). Friesen stresses that the Bible clearly reveals God's moral will for our lives—to become like Christ, to obey what is commanded, and so forth—and that the Bible offers wisdom for discerning what we should do in the real life situations, big and small.

Hontz, Marilyn. *Listening for God: How an Ordinary Person Can Learn to Hear God Speak* (Carol Stream, IL: Tyndale, 2004). Hontz emphasizes the Bible, journaling, and looking for everyday miracles as ways to hear God's voice

Huggett, Joyce. *The Joy of Listening to God* (Downer's Grove, IL: IVP Books, 1987). This well-loved classic focuses mostly on contemplative prayer as a way to listen to God. (A revised edition was published in 2006 by Hoddard and Stoughton with the title *Listening to God*. It includes one new chapter.)

Olsen, Charles M. *Transforming Church Boards into Communities of Spiritual Leaders* (Herndon, VA: The Alban Institute, 1995). Olsen has included significant material on communal discernment, giving a model for discernment that includes story-telling and listening.

Smith, Gordon T. *Listening to God's Will in Times of Choice: The Art of Discerning God's Will* (Downer's Grove, IL: IVP Books, 1997). Smith focuses on hearing God's voice in order to discern God's will for individuals. He gives a helpful explanation of how to draw on the wisdom of others in discernment.

Waltke, Bruce K. *Finding the Will of God: A Pagan Notion?* (Grand Rapids, MI: Eerdmans, 1995). Waltke is concerned that many Christians use hunches or superstitious practices when they try to discern God's will for them as individuals. He presents a balanced view on how to rely on the Bible and the Holy Spirit in seeking to hear God's voice.

Zimmer, Donald E. *Leadership and Listening: Spiritual Foundations for Church Governance* (Herndon, VA: The Alban Institute, 2011). "Listening" in the title refers to listening to God, in order to move away from church governance based on a business model toward an understanding of leadership as a response to God's guidance and presence.

BOOKS ON OTHER TOPICS MENTIONED IN THIS BOOK

Baab, Lynne M. *Joy Together: Spiritual Practices for Your Congregation* (Louisville, KY: Westminster John Knox Press, 2012). I focus on six specific spiritual practices and illustrate the way small groups or whole congregations can engage in them communally. I also have a chapter on receptivity, and I address some criticisms of spiritual practices.

Branson, Mark Lau. *Memories, Hopes, and Conversations: Appreciative Inquiry and Congregational Change* (Herndon, VA: The Alban Institute, 2004). The process of appreciative inquiry involves listening within a congregation, in response to questions about the congregation's strengths. Branson illustrates the process well.

Johnson, Abigail. *Reflecting with God* (Herndon, VA: The Alban Institute, 2004). Johnson recommends shared storytelling, and theological reflection on those stories, as a way to help small group members see the connections between their faith and their daily lives.

Moschella, Mary Clark. *Ethnography as Pastoral Practice: An Introduction* (Cleveland, OH: Pilgrim Press, 2008). Moschella advocates that pastors listen deeply to the stories of individuals within a congregation as well as the congregation's story as told in various forms by different individuals.

Pohl, Christine. *Making Room: Recovering Hospitality as a Christian Tradition* (Grand Rapids, MI: Eerdmans, 1999). The book that changed my understanding of ministry and motivated me to seek to be hospitable to everyone I meet, which nurtured a commitment to listening skills.

Pollock, Doug. *God Space: Where Spiritual Conversations Happen Naturally* (Loveland, CO: Group Publishing, 2009). Pollock is an evangelism coach, and his desire is to help readers increase the quality and quantity of their spiritual conversations. His approach is respectful and caring and involves a great deal of listening.

Rouse, Rick and Craig Van Gelder. *A Field Guide for the Missional Congregation: Embarking on a Journey of Transformation* (Minneapolis: Augsburg Fortress, 2008). Craig Van Gelder has written and edited numerous books on the missional church. This one is among the most practical, helping congregational leaders understand the issues and make positive changes within a congregation, which includes a move in the direction of listening to God.

Roxburgh, Alan J. *Missional Mapmaking: Skills for Leading in Times of Transition* (San Francisco: Jossey Bass, 2010). Roxburgh writes frequently about the missional church, and in this book discusses strategies and perspectives that enable leaders to change congregational culture in the direction of listening to God.

Standish, N. Graham. *Humble Leadership: Being Radically Open to God's Guidance and Grace* (Herndon, VA: The Alban Institute, 2007). Standish argues for humility, based in paying attention to God's presence in ourselves and others, as a key leadership attribute.

ABOUT THE AUTHOR

Lynne M. Baab has written numerous books for congregational leaders, including *Personality Type in Congregations*, *Reaching Out in a Networked World*, and *Beating Burnout in Congregations*. She has also written widely on Christian spiritual practices, including *Sabbath Keeping* and *Fasting*. Her most recent book, *Joy Together: Spiritual Practices for Your Congregation*, combines these two threads by describing the way small groups and whole congregations can engage in spiritual practices together. Lynne has also written several novels—murder mysteries with connections to congregations—published for kindle and other e-book formats. She is a Presbyterian Church (U.S.A.) minister who served two congregations in Seattle in associate roles. Her master of divinity degree is from Fuller Theological Seminary, and in 2007 she earned a PhD in communication from the University of Washington, focusing her research on the ways congregations present their identities and exercise persuasion on their websites. Since the completion of her doctoral studies, Lynne has been the Jack Somerville Lecturer in Pastoral Theology at the University of Otago in Dunedin, New Zealand. She is also an adjunct tutor at the Knox Centre for Ministry and Leadership, where ministers for the Presbyterian Church in Aotearoa, New Zealand, are trained. She is a frequent guest blogger for The Thoughtful Christian, Kiwi-Made Preaching and Godspace blogs. She lives with her husband, a watercolor artist, in Dunedin, New Zealand, and their two sons live in Seattle and Berlin.